Inspirational Football GOATS Stories, Amazing Facts, and Trivia Games

The Ultimate Football Gift Book for Kids and Teens!

Harris Baker

Contents

Introduction — V

The Legendary Football Heroes Biographies!

    Patrick Mahomes — 3

    The Kelce Brothers — 13

    Tom Brady — 23

    Peyton Manning — 34

    Larry Fitzgerald — 45

    Jerry Rice — 55

    Reggie White — 65

    Joe Montana — 75

Amazing Facts, Records, and Moments

    Origins and Early Evolution — 87

    The Field, Ball, and Stadiums — 90

    Rules and Gameplay — 93

    Roles on the Field — 96

    Leagues Organization — 99

    Historic Rivalries — 102

    Record-Breaking Players and Coaches — 105

Football Brain Games And Trivia!

    Game 1 - Touchdown True-or-False — 111

    Game 2 - Position Pairs Challenge — 113

Game 3 - Score It Right	115
Game 4 - Word Scramble	117
Game 5 - Name that NFL Team!	119
Game 6 - Penalty Decoder	121
Solutions - Basketball Brain Games And Trivia!	
Game 1 - Touchdown True-or-False (Solution)	124
Game 2 - Position Pairs Challenge (Solution)	126
Game 3 - Score It Right (Solution)	127
Game 4 - Word Scramble (Solution)	128
Game 5 - Name that NFL Team! (Solution)	130
Game 6 - Penalty Decoder (Solution)	132
Afterword	133
Also by Harris Baker	134

Introduction

Hey there, future football fans! Welcome to the ultimate gridiron adventure. Whether you're dreaming of game-winning touchdowns or just curious about the magic of the sport, this book has something for you.

Get ready to meet some of the most legendary players in football history—like Aaron Donald, Patrick Mahomes, and Jerry Rice. These stars dominated the field and redefined what it means to be great. But that's not all. We'll uncover jaw-dropping facts, the wildest records, and even dive into the quirks of football's history (like how the rules have changed over time!).

And for those who love a challenge, we've packed in brain-busting trivia and games. From riddles to word scrambles, you'll tackle puzzles that put your football knowledge to the test.

Ready to kick off the fun? Let's dive in!

Harris Baker

Copyright © 2024 by Harris BAKER

All rights reserved.

No portion of this book may be reproduced in any form without written permission from the publisher or author except as permitted by U.S. copyright law.

The Legendary Football Heroes Biographies !

Patrick Mahomes

THE KID WHO TURNED BACKYARD DREAMS INTO NFL MAGIC

In Tyler, Texas, where backyards and fields fill with warm sunshine, kids play every game like it's the biggest one ever, kicking up dust as they run and laugh with all their might. In that same town, there grows up a kid who takes every game to another level: Little Patrick. And let me tell you, he's not your average, run-of-the-mill kid. From day one, this boy is wild about sports. We're talking baseball, basketball, football, even a little backyard ping-pong action – basically, if it has a ball, Patrick wants to play. You know how most little kids can barely throw a baseball across the yard without it plopping down halfway?

Well, Patrick isn't that kid. At his very first T-ball practice, he grabs the ball at shortstop, winds up, and absolutely launches it to first base. BOOM. The ball hits the poor first baseman right in the face, shattering his glasses and probably his dignity a little bit.

Everyone else definitely knows he's different. By the end of that practice, the coach has had enough. Patrick's arm is so powerful, he basically gets banned from shortstop for the rest of the season. "Kid, from now on, you're only allowed to roll the ball to first base," the coach tells him, rubbing his temples like he's trying to fend off a headache. Patrick just grins, ready to play wherever. The coaches finally move him to catcher, hoping that'll keep him out of trouble. It doesn't. Patrick's competitive fire is like this uncontrollable beast, and once it's unleashed, it doesn't settle down.

And if you think Patrick's got intense energy, his friends are right there with him. These guys are the East Texas Crew – a tight-knit group of young athletes who practically live on the baseball diamond, basketball court, and football field. They're all pretty serious about sports, too, but even they know Patrick is on a whole other level. "We all knew that Pat, he had a chance to make it," says Ryan, one of Patrick's best friends. Ryan actually hears about Patrick before he even meets him, because there's this buzz around town about "the kid in Tyler." Soon enough, they're inseparable, practically living in each other's driveways and backyards. When they're not on an actual team, they make up their own games – tackle football, driveway basketball, and the legendary trampoline basketball at Jake Parker's house. Now, trampoline basketball might sound harmless, but trust me, it's anything but. As Patrick's friend Coleman Patterson says, "Somebody's getting dunked on. And then somebody's getting upset and trying to dunk on someone else."

Patrick isn't one to back down. This kid's idea of a casual backyard game is going all out like it's the championship finals. If he loses, he's immediately demanding a rematch. If he wins, he's setting up another round to make sure everyone knows it wasn't a fluke. "There were some things we played just for fun," says Cheatham. "But there would definitely be moments I was like, Dang! this dude wants to win as much as possible.'" Patrick's friends start calling it his "competitive juice," and they all know he's got more of it than anyone.

One of Patrick's all-time favorite moments happens at a basketball camp when he's just eight years old. The game is almost over, and the other team sinks what looks like the winning shot. One of Patrick's teammates starts heading to the bench, all sad and defeated, Patrick isn't having it. He calls for the in-bounds pass, takes two quick dribbles, and then launches a one-handed shot from three-quarters court, just before the buzzer. SWISH. The ball goes in! Patrick nails the shot like he's throwing a mini Hail Mary pass across the gym. But then, here's the catch. Since he's playing with the older kids, the game doesn't count three-pointers, so his epic, impossible shot only scores two points. The game goes to overtime... and, yeah, they end up losing in overtime. Can you imagine! Patrick can't stand it. He stomps off the court, shaking his head. Even at eight years old, he hates losing, and he's not about to forget it anytime soon.

His mom, Randi, tries to keep some kind of order in the house, but with Patrick around, it's like trying to tame a whirlwind. Her big rule? No throwing balls in the house. That lasts about five minutes before another ball starts flying all over the house. Patrick's got a football in one hand, a baseball in the other, and he's watching TV, casually tossing balls off the screen while pretending he's paying attention to whatever show is on. "I throw it off the TV because I was watching TV at the same time," he says, almost like he's proud of how much he's testing her patience. His mom is constantly yelling at him to stop, but Patrick's just grinning. The only miracle is he never actually breaks the screen. And he tells people proudly, "I never broke a screen." For Patrick, that's like a badge of honor – as if proving he's got crazy aim even when he's distracted.

And then there's baseball. His dad, Pat Mahomes Sr., is a former Major League pitcher, and Patrick grows up idolizing the game. He even picks up his dad's habit of sticking his tongue out when he throws – a detail that will stick with him all the way into his NFL career. His friends like to joke that he practically lives with a baseball in his hand. "He used to think he was Alex Rodriguez," his mom says, laughing. Back when his dad played for the Texas Rangers, little Patrick would trail around the field, wearing Rodriguez's number 13, pretending he's the Yankees shortstop himself. He even dresses up as A-Rod for Halloween one year, complete with a pair of Rodriguez's batting gloves and sunglasses. The whole "Showtime" persona is already brewing.

When Patrick finally gets old enough to play competitive baseball, he's terrifying. His friends know what's coming as soon as he takes the mound. "For one, he threw so hard," says Jake, who later ends up on Patrick's team. "You could barely see the ball coming at you while you were hitting." Imagine standing there, trying to hit a pitch from Patrick when you're only eleven years old, and he's whipping the ball at speeds that make you want to duck and cover like an asteroid zooming toward you from outer space. The kid's a fireballer, but he's also a little wild. His buddy Cheatham says "He is wild as crap," laughing. So it's not just that Patrick throws hard; it's that he might not know exactly where the ball's going either. Catchers get blisters trying to hold onto his pitches. His buddy Jake ends up having to wear a batting glove under his catcher's mitt just to survive.

By the time Patrick Mahomes hits high school at Whitehouse in East Texas, he's already something of a local legend, blowing minds on the baseball diamond, the basketball court, and more and more on the football field. Baseball has always been front and center—it's what his dad played professionally and what everyone expects him to follow. But football is starting to pull him in deeper: the thrill of a perfect spiral, slinging the ball across the field like a laser, juking a defender out of his cleats... it's all adding up to something special. Little by little, football becomes the sport—the one that feels just right. He juggles practices for all three sports and still has the energy to hang out with his friends afterward. His favorite part about playing so many sports? "It teaches me how to compete. It teaches me how to make things happen, how to make adjustments on the fly." Whether he drains a buzzer-beater in basketball or whips a no-look pass in football, it's all about split-second decision-making. In Patrick's mind, every move stays unpredictable, almost like a magic trick. One minute he zigs left; the next, he zags right. His friends never know what he'll do next—only that it'll be something wild and probably a little ridiculous, in the best possible way.

And by the time he joins the Whitehouse High School football team, it's clear to everyone that he's onto something big. He's lighting up the field in a way that makes people whisper, "This kid... he's different." He's not just the quarterback; he's a force. You can practically see the defense tense up whenever he steps back to throw. Mahomes has this effortless sidearm motion, honed from years of baseball, but now it's turned into a weapon on the football field. The stats he puts up sound like someone's made them up – 4,619 passing yards, 50 touchdowns in his senior year alone. And then, as if that's not enough, he adds 948 rushing yards and 15 more touchdowns just to keep things interesting.

But it's not all easy. Patrick's got the skills, but he's not exactly the most hyped recruit coming out of high school. People know he's talented, but he's only rated as a three-star recruit. In Texas – where football is practically a religion – three stars feels like an insult.

But Patrick doesn't get discouraged. Instead, he doubles down on his training, pushing himself to keep improving. He doesn't let rankings or scouting reports define him. Instead, he focuses on his love of the game, saying, "The biggest thing for me is just to go out there and win." And he plays every game with that attitude, like he's got something to prove, not just to recruiters, but to himself.

But here's the wild part – even though everyone thinks football is the thing for Patrick, he's still out there blowing people's minds in basketball and baseball too. It's like he's got this secret stash of energy no one else has. One minute, he's throwing touchdowns under the Friday night lights, and the next, he's back on the basketball court, playing like it's his main sport. Picture this: it's a packed crowd for Whitehouse's big basketball game against their arch-rival, John Tyler High. The crowd's buzzing, the tension's thick, and Patrick comes flying down the court on a fast break. Most high school kids in that situation would go for a safe layup, Patrick takes off from near the free-throw line, puts the ball behind his head, and absolutely posterizes the poor kid under the basket. The gym erupts. People are running up and down the stands, screaming like they've just seen Michael Jordan in his prime. Ryan, his friend, still laughs about it, saying, "I don't think I've ever seen him dunk a basketball – but he comes down on a fast break, with the defender basically on the block, and Pat takes off and dunks on this kid. The entire gym goes crazy."

When he's not dunking on people, Patrick's on the baseball diamond, making life very difficult for anyone who has to step up to the plate against him. His fastball is the stuff of nightmares, a blazing pitch that leaves his opponents squinting to even *see* the ball, much less hit it. Once, he throws a no-hitter with 16 strikeouts in a single game, and his friends joke that he might've been throwing faster than some college pitchers. But he's not just about power. Patrick's got *accuracy*, too – a skill that he'll later bring to the football field. Coleman Patterson, his baseball teammate, swears he never saw Patrick strike out. "If it happened, I don't remember it," he says, almost baffled, like he's still trying to wrap his head around how anyone could be *that* good.

It's clear that Patrick's got options. In fact, the Detroit Tigers select him in the 37th round of the MLB draft straight out of high school. That's right – he's got a shot to go pro in baseball right then and there. But by this point, Patrick's fallen in love with football, and he's not ready to give it up. So he makes a decision that will shape his entire future: he turns down the Tigers' offer and commits to play football and baseball at Texas Tech. The thing about Patrick is that he's *always* focused on the big picture, and right now, his big picture includes touchdowns, not home runs.

Once he arrives at Texas Tech, he's got to start from scratch again, this time as the backup quarterback behind Davis Webb. Now, a lot of guys in his position might get frustrated, but Patrick keeps his head down and works. He's got this quiet confidence that tells him his moment will come. Sure enough, when Webb goes down with an injury, Patrick steps up. His first big test comes against *Baylor*, and he doesn't hold back. He puts on an absolute clinic, throwing for a record-breaking 598 yards and six touchdowns. Suddenly, everyone's talking about the freshman with the cannon arm and the nerves of steel.

Over the next few years, he becomes a star at Texas Tech, turning heads with insane passing stats and his fearless playstyle. His sophomore year, he's putting up over 4,600 passing yards and 36 touchdowns. It's like watching a human highlight reel. Patrick's not *just* making big plays; he's doing it with style, throwing no-look passes and juking defenders out of their cleats. The local fans start calling him "Showtime," and honestly, it fits. Watching Patrick play is like watching a magic show – you know he's about to do something incredible, but you have no idea *what* it'll be.

By his junior year, Patrick's ready to take things to the next level. He decides to focus entirely on football, leaving baseball behind. And from that moment on, it's like a switch flips. He's all in. That season, he has a game against Oklahoma that goes down in college football history. Patrick throws for an *unbelievable* 734 yards, tying the NCAA single-game record. He racks up 819 total yards of offense in that game – *819*! Just to put that in perspective, that's more yards than some entire teams manage in a game. By the time the final whistle blows, people are shaking their heads in disbelief, and scouts around the country are starting to pay serious attention.

But for Patrick, it's not just about breaking records. He's got this mindset where every single play matters. he explains that "You have to learn and develop from every experience you see on the field," and he says "I might see an unscouted blitz, I might see different coverages than I'm expecting, so I need to process and make those adjustments as I go." He studies film like a scientist, dissecting every detail, every pattern, every tendency of the defense. He's learning the game on a level most players don't even *attempt*, and it's clear that he's not just preparing to *play* football – he's getting ready to take over the game.

Off the field, Patrick's got this laid-back vibe that makes him easy to root for. He's still close with his friends from high school, and they come out to support him whenever they can. To them, he's still the kid from Tyler who never backs down from a challenge. They call him up before big games, texting him funny GIFs on Instagram and hyping him up. And even though he's got all the pressure of being a college star, he stays grounded. He credits his faith for keeping him calm under pressure, saying, "Faith is huge for me... Before every game, I walk the field and I do a prayer at the goalpost." For Patrick, it's not about fame or stats; it's about staying true to himself and his values.

By the end of his junior year, Patrick has taken Texas Tech by storm. He's not just a college athlete anymore – he's a phenom. NFL scouts are flocking to Lubbock to watch him play, and he's becoming one of the most talked-about quarterbacks in the country. The coaches and analysts can't believe what they're seeing. Here's this kid who grew up idolizing Alex Rodriguez, who played every sport under the sun, and who's now redefining what a college quarterback can do. Patrick himself? He's calm, collected, and laser-focused.

When Patrick finally declares for the NFL Draft after his breakout junior year at Texas Tech, he's already become the talk of the town among scouts, coaches, and analysts. His arm strength, his mobility, his *wild* style of play – they're all the stuff of legend at this point, even though he hasn't played a single professional snap. Scouts say he's got "raw talent," but the kind that comes with a warning label: this kid is like a firework. You have no idea what's going to happen when he lights up, but you *know* it's going to be wild. And while some teams aren't sure if they're ready for that level of unpredictability, one team is ready to go *all in* on Patrick Mahomes: the Kansas City Chiefs.

Kansas City doesn't just *pick* Patrick. They *move mountains* to get him. The Chiefs trade up from the 27th to the 10th pick, giving up a handful of valuable picks in the process, because they're convinced they've found their guy. General Manager Brett Veach has been raving about Patrick since his college days, practically sprinting back to his office after every Texas Tech game to rewatch Mahomes' highlights. To him, this isn't just a gamble – it's a game-changer. And Coach Andy Reid? He's practically *salivating* at the chance to work with someone as creative and unpredictable as Mahomes. Reid, who's known for designing plays that look more like puzzles, sees Patrick as the missing piece – a quarterback who doesn't just think outside the box but *lives* outside of it.

In 2017, Patrick isn't stepping in as the main guy just yet. The Chiefs already have a solid, experienced quarterback in Alex Smith, and Reid makes it clear that Patrick's job for his rookie season is to learn, grow, and absorb as much as he can from the sidelines. For some players, this might feel like a disappointment. Patrick takes it in stride, understanding that he's got a unique opportunity to learn from one of the sharpest minds in the game. He says, "You have to learn and develop from every experience you see on the field." And that's what he does, studying Alex's every move, every read, every subtle fake. He watches the way Smith handles pressure, the way he keeps his cool, and Patrick learns.

Now, don't think that Patrick spends his rookie year quietly. Even if he's not on the field every Sunday, he's *making waves* in practice. Chiefs defensive legends like Derrick Johnson and Justin Houston start talking about this rookie quarterback who keeps making insane throws against them in drills. Johnson, a 13-year NFL veteran, says, "I never had a scout team quarterback beat me as consistently as he did." He's so good that the defenders think he's showing off – throwing no-look passes, threading impossible angles, and making it look *easy*. Johnson admits, "I actually got upset, thought he was hot-dogging around by looking this way and throwing the ball that way. But that was him. That was what he does, the way he plays."

Even Andy Reid gets caught off guard. One day at practice, Patrick throws a *no-look* pass right in front of him, something he's been secretly practicing. Reid stops, squints at Patrick, and just smiles, like he's thinking, "Did he really just do that?" It's as if Reid can already see the future. He knows that when Patrick finally steps onto the NFL stage, it's going to be something the league has never seen.

Then, in Week 17, the Chiefs have already clinched a playoff spot, and Reid decides it's time to unleash the rookie. He gives Patrick his first career start against the Denver Broncos. Now, playing in Denver as a rookie? That's no joke. The stadium's loud, the altitude messes with your breathing, and the Broncos' defense is as tough as they come. But Patrick walks in with that same grin, that same *Showtime* confidence. He completes 22 of 35 passes, racks up 284 yards, and leads the Chiefs to a thrilling 27-24 victory. Even though he throws an early interception – a classic rookie mistake – he shrugs it off and finishes the game like a veteran. His teammate Mitchell Schwartz remembers it well: "He didn't get intimidated by the moment… That kind of solidified his status and his ability to lead a team in the future."

The Chiefs' locker room is buzzing. It's like everyone suddenly *gets it*. This isn't just a kid with a cannon arm and a flashy style. This is a quarterback who can handle pressure, who makes plays in the clutch, who isn't fazed by the big stage. Brett, the General Manager of the Kansas City Chiefs, watching from the press box, says, "That was probably the moment where we all knew… he was destined to do some pretty good things."

And then comes 2018. The Chiefs trade Alex Smith, officially naming Patrick their starting quarterback, and from the *very first game*, he's an absolute sensation. In Week 1, he throws *four* touchdowns against the Los Angeles Chargers, putting on a show that has everyone in the NFL scrambling for popcorn. The next week, he tops himself with a *six-touchdown game* against the Pittsburgh Steelers. SIX TOUCHDOWNS in two games, he's thrown for ten touchdowns, breaking records left and right, and making defensive coordinators around the league *panic*. He says "You want to make the big play; you want to throw a touchdown every single play, but at the same time, you have to know that it's a process." And Patrick *perfects* that process, one play at a time.

He's having a season straight out of a superhero story: 5,097 passing yards, 50 touchdowns, and a passer rating that's so high it makes even the top players stop and stare! Patrick's only the second quarterback in NFL history to hit 5,000 yards and 50 touchdowns in one season, joining the legendary Peyton Manning in this super-elite club. When the regular season wraps up, he's crowned league MVP, the first Kansas City Chief to ever win it! Chiefs fans are in total shock, watching this kid rocket from a backup to a superstar in just one season.

And here's the best part. He also has this spark, this buzz that you can feel even if you're sitting way up in the nosebleed seats! He's throwing no-look passes, dodging defenders like he's got eyes in the back of his head, and launching throws across his body like it's a backyard game. It's like that kid from East Texas—the one who practiced by throwing at the TV and dunking on his friends in the driveway—has jumped straight onto the NFL field. He loved playing together with his teammates. As he says, 'The team aspect of football and just playing quarterback, having the ball in your hands, making the plays—that was always my favorite.' And you can tell! Every snap, every pass, he's bringing that same fearless energy, giving the game everything he's got!

When the playoffs roll around, Patrick leads the Chiefs to their first home playoff win in *over 25 years* with a 31-13 victory over the Indianapolis Colts. The entire city of Kansas City is on fire with excitement. But in the AFC Championship Game against the New England Patriots, Patrick and the Chiefs fall just short, losing in heartbreaking overtime. It's a tough moment for him, but instead of feeling defeated, he sees it as motivation. "You have to learn and develop from every experience you see on the field," he said. For Patrick, even a loss is a stepping stone to something bigger.

And then comes 2019—the year Patrick Mahomes goes from MVP to straight-up legend! After an unforgettable season, he leads the Chiefs back to the playoffs. In the Divisional Round against the Houston Texans, things look bleak. The Chiefs are down 24-0 in the first half, and it seems like the game might be over. But not with Patrick. He fires up his team, leading them to score a jaw-dropping seven touchdowns in a row, pulling off one of the most unbelievable comebacks in NFL history! The Chiefs storm to victory with a final score of 51-31, and Patrick's legend reaches new heights!

And now, the ultimate goal is right there—the Super Bowl! The air crackles with energy as Patrick leads the Chiefs into Super Bowl LIV against the San Francisco 49ers. The stadium roars with every snap, every play, as if the whole world is watching. The battle is fierce, and the Chiefs find themselves down 20-10 in the fourth quarter. The tension is so thick you can almost feel it pressing down on the field. But if you think Patrick is backing down, you're in for a shock! With less than seven minutes left, he steps up, eyes sharp, heart pounding, and takes command. He launches a touchdown pass that slices through the air like a rocket, sparking an eruption of cheers from the stands. Then, another—each play a surge of adrenaline, a game-changer that has fans on their feet, screaming. The comeback is epic, the kind that leaves jaws dropping and chills racing down spines. The Chiefs take it 31-20, and as the confetti rains down, Patrick lifts the Super Bowl MVP trophy, making history as the youngest quarterback to ever claim that honor.

As the confetti rains down, he's got that signature grin on his face, holding the Lombardi Trophy high. It's a moment that feels like destiny. After years of backyard football, high school heroics, college shootouts, and countless hours of practice, Patrick has reached the pinnacle of his sport. And who knows what's next? All we know is that wherever he goes, he's taking that same competitive juice, that unstoppable energy, and that Texas-sized love of the game with him. One thing's for sure – this is only the beginning of Showtime Mahomes. And if this is the start, then we're all in for one heck of a show.

The Kelce Brothers

Two Tornadoes, One Epic Journey

Travis Kelce and Jason Kelce grew up in Cleveland Heights, Ohio, a place where, if you asked their mom Donna, the phrase "never a dull moment" was probably invented. The streets were lined with tall, leafy trees, and the houses were old but full of character—just like the Kelce household, which always seemed to be in a state of mild chaos. Their mom used to sip her morning coffee while keeping an ear out for the next crash or shriek. These two boys were like little tornadoes, spinning through the house, breaking windows, crashing into walls, and driving their parents absolutely bananas. "I didn't raise boys. I raised demolition crews," Donna says, half-joking, half-serious. But hey, if breaking things was an Olympic sport, the Kelce brothers would've earned gold medals.

Jason, born on November 5, 1987, was the serious older brother—the type of kid who probably thought about consequences before doing something, but then did it anyway because Travis dared him to. He had a habit of furrowing his brow in concentration when he was about to do something risky, as if weighing the pros and cons before ultimately shrugging and going for it. Travis, born two years later on October 5, 1989, was the quintessential little brother. You know the type—wild, mischievous, and powered by pure chaos. He was the kid who'd poke a hornet's nest just to see what would happen, cackling with delight even as he sprinted away. Their dad, Ed, summed it up best: "Travis? He was the instigator. Jason? He was the one cleaning up the mess." The dynamic was crystal clear every time someone heard a crash in the living room, followed by Jason's voice yelling, "Travis, what did you do?!"

Their competitive streak began early. Donna described them as being in a constant race. "Who could get to the table first? Who could eat faster? Who could throw the first punch?" The kitchen table bore endless scratches and dents from their wrestling over bowls of cereal. Yes, punches were thrown, but not the kind that land you in trouble (well, not always). It was the kind of brotherly battle that built character—and occasionally ended with one of them sitting in timeout, arms folded, refusing to make eye contact with the other.

It's in preschool that things got really wild. Jason and Travis weren't model kids. They both got kicked out. Yes, you read that right—kicked out of preschool. Jason got expelled after a cafeteria-table duel involving sporks. As he admitted, "We were stabbing each other with sporks, and I guess I got carried away. The other kid ended up with four little dots on his forehead. Not my proudest moment." In the retelling, Jason can't help but chuckle at how silly it was that a couple of toddlers managed to turn sporks into miniature swords.

Travis, on the other hand, got the boot because of his refusal to share a checkers set. "I kept winning," Travis said. "And the teacher was like, 'You have to share,' and I was like, 'No, I don't.'" When she insisted, Travis launched the chair he was sitting in across the room. Classic Travis. Jason still teases him about it: "Who gets kicked out of preschool for checkers? Travis Kelce, that's who." Donna once remarked that she wasn't sure if she should be proud or slightly horrified at her youngest's competitive spirit even then.

Their competitive streak didn't mellow out as they got older. By elementary school, they were already staging wrestling matches in the living room, much to Donna's despair. "I stopped buying nice furniture," she confessed. One time, Travis convinced Jason to try out a new move he called the "Super Slam Dunkinator." It involved jumping off the couch and landing on Jason, who was sprawled out on a beanbag chair. The beanbag chair exploded in a flurry of tiny foam beads that clung to everything—hair, clothes, even the walls—and their dad Ed walked in just in time to see stuffing raining down like snowflakes.

"Travis!" Ed yelled, momentarily stunned by the storm of beanbag stuffing floating around the living room. Jason, ever the diplomat, tried to take the blame. "It was both of us!" he said. But Ed knew better. He fixed Travis with a look saying, "I know this was your idea."

Things escalated when the boys got their first set of bikes. They turned the quiet neighborhood streets into their personal BMX stunt park. Jason, ever the rule-follower, wore a helmet and rode cautiously, carefully checking to make sure his laces were tucked in so they wouldn't get caught. Travis, helmet-less and fearless, was the kid who'd yell, "Watch this!" before crashing into a bush. Once, he tried to jump over a makeshift ramp Jason built out of plywood and cinderblocks. The ramp collapsed mid-jump, and Travis landed face-first in the grass.

Donna came running out, yelling, "What were you thinking?!" as she plucked a tangle of weeds out of his hair. "I was thinking it'd work," Travis replied, picking twigs out of his elbows too.

By the time they hit middle school, the brothers had added sports to their list of competitive outlets. They played everything—football, basketball, baseball, even lacrosse. Jason dabbled in hockey too, because why not? But football was where they really shined. At recess, they'd turn the playground into a mini gridiron, with Travis launching spirals and Jason plowing through anyone who got in his way. And being honest, Travis couldn't resist any opportunity to tackle Jason, even if it wasn't technically part of the game. Their teachers and classmates could barely keep track of their endless contests—who could climb the monkey bars fastest, who could do the most pull-ups, who could run laps around the yard without getting winded.

At home, their fights weren't confined to sports. They fought over the TV remote, who got the last slice of pizza, and—most importantly—who got the front seat in the car.

Donna eventually solved the problem by implementing a strict "odd days, even days" system. "If it's an odd day, Jason gets the front seat. If it's an even day, Travis does." Travis wasn't thrilled. "What if I feel like an odd day on an even day?" he argued, crossing his arms in protest. Donna didn't budge. She kept a little calendar on the kitchen fridge, meticulously marking each day so there was no confusion about whose turn it was.

By high school, their competitive energy reached new heights. Travis was the quarterback on the football team, dazzling everyone with his arm and his legs. He had a flair for showmanship—he'd celebrate every touchdown by spinning the ball or flashing a grin at the crowd. Jason, meanwhile, played linebacker and fullback, crushing opponents with his no-nonsense approach to the game. He was the kind of player who'd clench his jaw and charge forward, knocking rivals aside like bowling pins. But school was a different game. During Jason's senior year, Travis failed French class and got benched. "How do you fail French?" Jason asked him, shaking his head. Travis shrugged. "I didn't conjugate the verbs or whatever. Plus, French fries are already in English, so what's the point?" he joked, tossing a football in the air as if the matter were trivial.

Jason, ever the supportive big brother, still wished they could've played that year together. But deep down, Travis didn't sweat it too much. He was too busy sneaking hot dogs into the locker room for post-practice snacks, flashing mischievous grins at Jason when he got away with it. The rest of the team figured out pretty quickly that if you were hungry, you found Travis.

Despite the occasional hiccup (or suspension), the Kelce brothers' high school days laid the foundation for their future greatness. As Travis says: "I think our competitiveness growing up is a big reason we both made it to the NFL." And Jason agreed, adding, "Yeah, but let's not forget who won most of those childhood fights."

"Excuse me?" Travis shot back. "Pretty sure I have a better win-loss record." "Debatable," Jason replied with a wry grin.

One thing's for sure: growing up Kelce meant nonstop action, endless laughter, and a whole lot of broken furniture. And if their memories are anything to go by, Cleveland Heights never quite recovered from the whirlwind that was Jason and Travis Kelce.

By the time Jason packed up his belongings—carefully folding his clothes into a beat-up duffel bag and tucking away a few prized football trophies from his high school days—and left Cleveland for the University of Cincinnati, he was ready to chart his own course. He could almost feel the weight of the moment as he closed the door to his childhood room, filled with faint echoes of backyard scrimmages and brotherly banter. After all, he was the older brother—the responsible one, the leader, the guy who didn't throw chairs at preschool teachers. Jason was walking on to the Bearcats football team, determined to make a name for himself. And for two blissful years, he thought he'd left behind the whirlwind of chaos known as Travis Kelce. But Travis? Oh, Travis had other plans.

In 2008, two years after Jason arrived, Travis rolled up to Cincinnati in a flurry of confident grins and exaggerated swagger. And let me tell you, he didn't quietly join the team. Travis entered like a human wrecking ball, equal parts talent and trouble. Jason should've known things were about to get wild when Travis chose to live with him. "I thought I'd have some peace and quiet," Jason joked, "but then he showed up." It didn't take long for Travis to fill their new shared space with his booming laughter, half-eaten pizza boxes, and a lively energy that buzzed around every corner of the apartment.

From the start, it was clear Travis was an incredible athlete. As a redshirt freshman, he played tight end and even stepped in as a Wildcat quarterback, scoring two rushing touchdowns. On the field, he moved like he had rockets in his cleats, leaving defenders stumbling in his wake. But off the field? That's where things got messy. Travis loved football, sure, but he also loved partying. A lot. He'd roll back into the apartment in the early morning hours, making a racket as he kicked off his shoes. He would even admit that he was having the time of his life, maybe too much fun.

Jason, meanwhile, was focused. By his senior year, he'd transitioned from linebacker to offensive lineman, earning a starting spot and catching the attention of scouts. He was the kind of guy who spent weekends studying playbooks and perfecting footwork drills. "I kept my head down, worked hard, and stayed out of trouble," Jason said. "Travis... not so much." Still, even amidst the late-night chaos Travis stirred up, there was a brotherly pride that flickered in Jason's eyes when he watched Travis tear it up on the field.

By the spring of 2010, when Travis's "fun" finally caught up with him. During routine NCAA postseason testing, Travis tested positive for marijuana. It was a gut punch—not just for him but for the entire Kelce family. He was suspended for the entire 2010 season, and worse, his scholarship was revoked. Jason got the call first. His baby brother was out of chances. And as much as Travis played the cool, carefree guy, this one hit him hard. "I was embarrassed," Travis says. "It was the first time I'd really felt like I let everyone down—my family, my teammates, myself."

Jason didn't waste time. He drove straight to Travis's dorm, barged in, and found his brother sitting on the floor surrounded by pizza boxes and empty Gatorade bottles. There was a defeated slump to Travis's shoulders, like he was carrying the weight of every mistake he'd ever made. "Dude," Jason said, exasperated, "what the hell are you doing?" Travis looked up, shrugged, and said, "Trying to figure out what's next."

Jason, always the big brother, didn't give up on him. He marched straight into the head coach's office—Butch Jones at the time—and pleaded with him. "Coach, don't give up on him. I'll keep an eye on him. I'll make sure he gets his act together," Jason promised. Somehow, Jason convinced Coach Jones to let Travis stay on the scout team while he worked on earning his spot back.

Travis moved in with Jason and Jason's teammates, a tight-knit group of offensive linemen whose idea of fun involved intense practice sessions and epic team dinners where plates of pasta could feed an army. "I basically babysat him," Jason jokes. Travis actually stepped up. He worked hard, stayed out of trouble, and even made the honor roll for the first time in his life. Nights that had once been filled with music blasting from speakers were now replaced by the hum of Travis tapping away at a keyboard, determined to keep his grades up. "Jason basically saved my career," Travis said, getting emotional. "I don't think I've ever properly thanked him for that." But make no mistake—living with Jason wasn't a walk in the park. Jason's nickname among his teammates was "The Sheriff," and he took that title seriously. Lights out by 10 p.m. No wild parties. No skipping class. One time, Travis tried to sneak out to a party, and Jason caught him climbing out the window. "Where do you think you're going?" Jason asked, arms folded with that stern older-brother glare. Travis froze. "Uh... checking the weather?" Jason dragged him back inside, grumbling, "You're not screwing this up again."

By 2011, Travis was reinstated on the team, and he came back with a vengeance. That season, he played tight end and hauled in 13 catches for 150 yards and two touchdowns. It wasn't flashy, but it was progress. Every time he stepped onto the field, there was a quiet fire in his eyes, a resolve forged from the lessons he'd learned. And more importantly, he stayed out of trouble. Jason, meanwhile, wrapped up his college career and prepared for the NFL Draft. But before he left, he pulled Travis aside and said, "You've got the talent. Now you've gotta act like it." In that moment, you could see the respect and determination radiating from Travis.

In 2012, with Jason now in the NFL, Travis finally had his breakout season. He racked up 45 receptions, 722 yards, and eight touchdowns, earning first-team all-conference honors and the College Football Performance Awards Tight End of the Year. He was officially on the radar of NFL scouts. But Travis wasn't just winning on the field—he was also winning off it. He graduated with a degree in Interdisciplinary Studies, making his mom Donna proud. "I didn't think I'd ever see the day," she joked. "But there he was, in a cap and gown. I nearly fainted." The photo of Travis, beaming in his graduation robe, remains a cherished family keepsake to this day.

Jason, now playing for the Philadelphia Eagles, couldn't have been prouder. "I always knew he had it in him," he said. "He just needed a little... encouragement. Or a lot." Even his playful jibes came with a warm undercurrent of admiration.

But even as they started carving out their own paths, the bond between Jason and Travis remained unbreakable. They called each other constantly, offering advice, trash talk, and support. Jason never let Travis forget about the time he bailed him out in college. "I should charge you rent for all those months I babysat you," Jason teased.

And Travis? He took it all in stride. "You didn't babysit me," he shot back. "You inspired me. There's a difference." You could almost hear Jason chuckling on the other end of the line, rolling his eyes in affectionate disbelief.

Their time at Cincinnati wasn't perfect—far from it. But those years shaped them into the men they would become. For Travis, it was a story of redemption. For Jason, it was a lesson in patience. And for both, it was a reminder that no matter how different they were, they'd always have each other's backs.

When Jason got the call in 2011 that he'd been drafted by the Philadelphia Eagles in the sixth round, he could barely contain his excitement. "Sixth round, 191st pick? Sounds like a steal to me," Jason said, laughing. But while Jason was packing his bags for Philly, his first thought wasn't about what jersey number he'd wear or where he'd live—it was about Travis. "I thought, 'Man, I hope this kid keeps his head on straight,'" Jason said. Travis had turned things around in college, but would he keep it going?

Fast-forward two years to 2013, and it was Travis's turn to hear his name called. The Kansas City Chiefs picked him in the third round, and when Andy Reid—who had coached Jason during his early Eagles days—called Travis, it was like a full-circle moment for the family. But Andy didn't sugarcoat things. "Listen," Coach Reid said, "you've got talent, but you've also got a reputation. Don't screw this up." Travis, never one to shy away from honesty, said, "Yes, sir. No funny business. Well, maybe a *little* funny business."

Jason, already grinding his way to becoming one of the NFL's best centers, immediately called Travis after the draft. "You're in good hands with Andy," Jason told him. "But don't embarrass me, alright?" Travis laughed. "Dude, I'm the *fun* Kelce. You're the boring one. Let me do my thing." And do his thing he did. Travis exploded onto the NFL scene—not immediately, of course, because in classic Kelce fashion, he had to overcome a knee injury that sidelined him for his rookie season. But by 2014, he was making highlight-reel plays, catching touchdowns, and dancing in the end zone like he was auditioning for *Dancing with the Stars*. "I wanted to let the league know I was here to stay," Travis said. "Also, I really like dancing."

Meanwhile, Jason was quietly becoming the anchor of the Eagles' offensive line. He didn't have the flashy moves or the camera-ready smile, but he had grit. Teammates described him as a workhorse, a leader, and, occasionally, a lumberjack—thanks to his signature bushy beard. "Jason's the type of guy who'll study game tape until 3 a.m.," one Eagles coach said. "Travis is the type of guy who'll send you a meme at 3 a.m."

Despite their different styles, the brothers remained close. They called each other after every game, win or lose. If Travis had a bad game, Jason would remind him to focus on the fundamentals. If Jason was frustrated after a loss, Travis would crack a joke to cheer him up. "He's my best friend," Jason said. "Even if he's a total goofball."

In 2017, Jason reached the pinnacle of his career: the Eagles won Super Bowl LII, beating Tom Brady and the New England Patriots. Jason celebrated the way only Jason could—by dressing up in a Mummers costume (basically a cross between a marching band outfit and a Vegas showgirl get-up) and delivering an epic, fiery speech at the Eagles' victory parade. "We wanted it more!" Jason roared to the crowd. Travis, watching from Kansas City, was equal parts proud and amused. "I saw that speech and thought, 'Wow, he's finally loosened up!'" Travis joked.

Not to be outdone, Travis earned his own Super Bowl ring in 2020 when the Chiefs defeated the San Francisco 49ers. True to form, Travis's post-game celebration involved quoting the Beastie Boys and leading the crowd in a raucous chant of "You gotta fight for your right to party!" Jason called him afterward and said, "I'm proud of you, man. But next time, maybe tone down the yelling?" Travis replied, "Never."

By 2023, the Kelce brothers had cemented their places as NFL legends, but they weren't done making history. On February 12, 2023, in a moment straight out of a Hollywood movie, the brothers faced off in Super Bowl LVII—Jason with the Eagles and Travis with the Chiefs. The world called it the "Kelce Bowl," but Donna, their mom, had a better name: "My Worst Nightmare Bowl." She showed up to the game in a custom-made split jersey—half Eagles, half Chiefs—and brought cookies for both boys. "She's Switzerland," Jason joked. "Neutral territory."

The game crackled with tension from the very first whistle, a swirling storm of roaring fans, bone-crunching hits, and hearts pounding so loud you could almost hear them. On one side of the field, Travis stood like a spark ready to ignite, eyes locked on the end zone, brimming with the kind of confidence that made it feel inevitable—*he* was going to make the play. Early in the first quarter, with the ball spiraling toward him, Travis leapt, snagged it mid-air, and barreled past defenders like a wrecking ball through drywall. As he crossed into the end zone, he spiked the ball so hard it bounced nearly back into orbit, turning to flash a triumphant, toothy grin that screamed, "How you like me now, big bro?" Across the field, Jason didn't flinch, his face a mask of determination. He wasn't here for glory—no touchdowns, no dances—but every block he made was a masterpiece of grit, a one-man fortress shielding his quarterback from the onslaught of Chiefs defenders. The game swayed back and forth, a heavyweight bout where every play felt like it could tip the scales, and in the end, it was the Chiefs who claimed victory, edging out the Eagles 38-35 in a finish so close it left fans clutching their chests like they'd run the field themselves.

As the final whistle blew and confetti exploded into the air, the Kelce brothers met at midfield, surrounded by chaos yet locked in their own quiet moment. Travis pulled Jason into a bear hug, his voice thick with emotion as he whispered, "You had a hell of a season." Jason, sweat streaked and exhausted but proud, nodded slowly, his voice steady even as his heart broke. "You earned this one, little bro." The words hung between them, a testament to a bond that no scoreline could ever change.

After the game, Donna made headlines for running onto the field to hug both sons. "It's the best day of my life and the worst day of my life," she told reporters. Ed, their dad, stayed in the background, proudly watching his sons make history. "They've come a long way since those backyard wrestling matches," he said. "Although Travis still celebrates like he's 10 years old."

The Kelce brothers weren't just stars on the field. Off the field, they were winning hearts and breaking the internet with their podcast, *New Heights*. Launched in 2022, the weekly show became a sensation as the brothers shared hilarious childhood stories, NFL insights, and ridiculous banter. One episode had them debating whether aliens lived in Antarctica. Travis argued, "Nobody goes there, so it's the perfect hiding spot." Jason replied, deadpan, "Nobody goes there because it's *Antarctica*." Fans couldn't get enough.

Their personal lives were just as full. Jason married Kylie McDevitt in 2018, and the couple had three daughters—with a fourth on the way. Travis, meanwhile, made headlines in 2023 when he started dating global superstar Taylor Swift. Suddenly, the Kelce brothers weren't just NFL icons—they were pop culture phenomena. "I guess I have to start liking her music now," Jason teased. Travis replied, "Don't lie. You've been singing 'Shake It Off' in the car for years."

As of 2024, Jason had retired from the NFL, transitioning into broadcasting with a new late-night sports show, while Travis was still chasing another Super Bowl ring with the Chiefs. But no matter where life took them, their bond remained unshakable. "At the end of the day, we're each other's biggest fans," Travis said. Jason added, "And biggest critics."

The Kelce brothers' journey from backyard brawls to NFL glory is a story of resilience, redemption, and, above all, brotherhood. They've shown the world that sibling rivalry can lead to greatness—so long as there's a lot of love, a little trash talk, and maybe a few broken windows along the way.

Tom Brady

A Scrappy Kid Story

Tom Brady's story begins on August 3, 1977, in the sunny town of San Mateo, California, where little Tommy Brady made his grand entrance into the world as the fourth child—and the *only* boy—of Galynn and Tom Brady Sr. He had three older sisters, Maureen, Julie, and Nancy, which meant he grew up surrounded by pink bikes, ballet recitals, and a whole lot of teasing. Some might say he had to learn to toughen up early, because having three big sisters is like playing defense against the Dallas Cowboys every single day. They could outwit, out-talk, and probably out-wrestle him if they wanted to.

The Brady family lived on Portola Drive, in a neighborhood that could've been straight out of a kid's adventure movie. Imagine streets filled with 42 kids, all under 16, running wild like a pack of sneakers and scraped knees. Tommy was one of the youngest, but he made up for it by being the most persistent. If there was a game—any game—Tommy wanted in. Capture the Flag? He was sprinting before you finished explaining the rules. Baseball in the street? Tommy was the one swinging for the fences, or, in this case, the nearest power line (a home run by neighborhood standards). If a ball went over someone's fence, Tommy was the kid knocking on doors asking, "Mr. and Mrs., can we please get the tennis ball back?"

His childhood best friend, Bobby, remembers Tommy as the kind of kid who never gave up. "We'd be playing football in the street, and Tommy was always shouting, 'Throw to me! Throw to me!' He didn't look like a wall or dart like an arrow, but boy, was he persistent. And if he lost? Forget it. He'd huff and puff like a cartoon character. But the next day, he'd be right back out there, ready to play again." It didn't matter if it was football, baseball, or who could eat the most jalapeños without crying (yes, they really did that at Pine Mountain Lake during family camping trips). Tommy always gave it 110 percent. One of his childhood friends, Scott, summed it up perfectly: "He hated to lose. Hated it. If he struck out or missed a throw, you'd think his whole day crumbled. But you know what? That's the same fire you see in him today."

It might surprise you to know that before football became the sun around which young Tommy's world revolved, his first true love was actually baseball. That's right—before touchdowns and Super Bowls, it was about swings and line drives. Back in the day, the neighborhood kids turned their street into a makeshift diamond with rules that would've made the MLB commissioner do a double take. A manhole cover served as home plate, and a fire hydrant marked the pitcher's mound. Hitting the ball past a particular tree? Home run. But if you were left-handed—like Tommy was in baseball—you had to master the art of pulling the ball, or risk it landing in someone's yard (and good luck getting it back). And breaking a window? Oh, breaking windows was practically their signature move—like, "Oops, we did it again!" Bobby laughs about it to this day: "We broke so many windows, we should've had a punch card for the local glass repair shop."

Amidst all the street games and neighborhood chaos, there was one thing that truly captured Tommy's brain: the San Francisco 49ers. Growing up in the shadow of Candlestick Park, the 49ers were the beating heart of the Bay Area, the stuff of legend. And for young

Tommy, they were magic. And one fateful day, that magic came to life. Tommy, just 4 years old, went with his family to Candlestick Park to watch the 49ers play in the NFC Championship. It was a cold day, and little Tommy was bundled up in a 49ers scarf and hat, his face sticky with hot chocolate. But none of that mattered when Montana threw "The Catch" to Dwight Clark, securing a 49ers victory against the Cowboys. The crowd erupted, and Tommy stared wide-eyed at the field, as if someone had just shown him the secret to happiness. He turned to his dad and shouted, "That's what I want to do!"

From that moment on, Joe Montana was Tommy's hero, his inspiration, his version of Superman. "I wanted to *be* Joe Montana," Tom has said. "Everything he did, I wanted to copy. He was the coolest guy on the planet."

As Tommy got older, he took that inspiration and channeled it into every aspect of his life. His sister Maureen, a star athlete herself, remembered how competitive he was even as a kid. "I'd be pitching tennis balls at him in the driveway—me, a high school All-American softball player—and he'd still manage to hit them over the house. He was 9 years old!"

While sports were undeniably a huge part of Tommy's childhood, life on Portola Drive wasn't *all* about touchdowns and home runs. Growing up in San Mateo in the '80s meant soaking in the kind of carefree, sunlit days that felt endless—days spent riding bikes to the local park, dreaming up wild new games with the neighborhood kids, and racing home as the streetlights flickered on. The Brady family wasn't flashy or extravagant, but what they lacked in luxury, they made up for with love, laughter, and togetherness. Tommy's mom, Galynn, had one rule that held firm no matter how exciting the game outside was: the family always ate dinner together. Even if it meant interrupting a heated street match, she'd stick her head out the door and holler, "Come on, Tommy, it's meatloaf night!" Tommy, of course, would groan like the world was ending, dragging his feet toward the table—but he always went, because in the Brady house, family came first.

One of the best parts about growing up was his dad's sense of humor. "My dad was always telling jokes," Tom has said. "I think I got my competitiveness from my mom, but my love of joking around? That's all Dad." For example, when little Tommy complained about not being big enough to tackle the older kids, Tom Sr. handed him a pillow and said, "Here, take this. It's called the *fear eliminator*." (the pillow didn't help much.)

Through it all, one thing became clear: Tommy was different. He wasn't built like a fortress or as fast as a flash, but he had something you couldn't measure—heart. He cared more, worked harder, and dreamed bigger than anyone else on the block. Even at a young age, he was the kid who stayed late after everyone else went home, practicing his throws in the fading light. He once said, "If you don't believe in yourself, why is anyone else going to believe in you?" That quote could've been his motto back then, because Tommy Brady—San Mateo's scrappy, competitive, never-give-up kid—believed he was destined for greatness. And you know what? He was absolutely right.

By the time Tommy Brady turned 14, he was ready to take his competitive streak to a new level. Gone were the days of hitting tennis balls over his family's roof or negotiating with Mr. and Mrs. So-and-So for a lost baseball. Now, Tommy walked through the doors of Junípero Serra High School in San Mateo with a swagger that said, "I've got big dreams, and no manhole-cover home plate can contain me." The place wasn't just any high school—it was already famous for producing great athletes, including Barry Bonds. Tommy thought, *If Barry can make it, why not me?*

Things didn't start out like a Hollywood sports movie though. In fact, Tommy's freshman year on the football team was more like a blooper reel. He joined as a backup quarterback on the junior varsity team, which—get this—had an 0–8 record and hadn't scored a single touchdown all year. *Not one touchdown.* The team couldn't score if the other team gave them a map and a flashlight. Tommy's job? Stand on the sideline, hold a clipboard, and wait for something—*anything*—to happen. But nothing did.

Tommy didn't give up. He watched. He learned. He studied the game like it was his ticket to the moon. "Things don't correct themselves; you've got to go out there and work hard to correct them," he would later say, and that's what he did. Day by day, throw by throw, he got better. By his sophomore year, he started getting more reps. And then, when the starting quarterback got injured, the coach finally looked at Tommy and said, "You're up."

Now, let me set the scene for you. Imagine a lanky kid, barely filling out his shoulder pads, jogging onto the field. His teammates weren't expecting much—this was the kid who used to carry water bottles, after all. But Tommy took that moment and ran with it. By the end of the season, he had earned the starting quarterback position for the varsity team. Cue the dramatic movie music.

By his junior year, Tommy Brady was officially QB1. He wasn't the most athletic kid on the field, but he had a brain for football that could rival Einstein's brain for equations. He could read defenses like a book and make throws that made coaches raise their eyebrows and say, "Hmm, maybe this kid's got something."

He also had a work ethic that made him stand out. After practice, when the field turned into a playground of laughter and hijinks, Tommy was the one staying late, throwing pass after pass, sometimes until it got so dark he could barely see his receiver. His dad, Tom Sr., liked to joke, "The lights at Serra stayed on a little longer because of my son."

Tommy's love for sports had always been boundless—if it had a ball, a bat, or even a flimsy set of made-up rules, he was all in. Remember that love for baseball? The same love that powered those childhood games on Portola Drive with manhole home plates and fire hydrant pitcher's mounds—followed Tommy into high school, but here's where things start to sound almost unreal. Tommy was still great at it, the kind of player scouts couldn't stop talking about. Think about it: the kid who would go on to become the greatest quarterback in NFL history also had the talent to play *professional baseball*. As the catcher for Serra's baseball team, Tommy was a left-handed dynamo with a cannon for an arm. "He could throw a ball so fast, it felt like it was leaving a vapor trail," one coach said. By the time he graduated, the Montreal Expos—the *Expos!*—drafted him in the 18th round of the 1995 MLB Draft, calling him a future All-Star. Let that sink in for a second: the greatest quarterback of all time was also good enough to have a professional baseball career. And yet, for all his remarkable talent behind the plate, Tommy's heart was somewhere else. "I love baseball," he said, "but you can't throw touchdowns in baseball." As dazzling as his baseball prospects were, Tommy already knew where he truly belonged—on a football field, chasing dreams no one else could see yet.

Let's not skip over how much work it took for Tommy to get noticed by college scouts for football. Back in the early 1990s, high school recruiting wasn't the high-tech operation it is today. No Twitter highlights, no viral YouTube clips. If you wanted a college to notice you, you had to go old-school: VHS tapes. Tommy and his dad sat down with a stack of blank VHS tapes, picked out the best plays from his games, and mailed them to colleges across the country. Think about that—he *mailed* them. If a scout wanted to watch Tommy play, they had to find a VCR first. And guess what? It worked.

Colleges started calling, and Tommy had options. His dad secretly hoped he'd stay close to home and play for Cal-Berkeley, but Tommy had other ideas. After weighing his choices—Cal, UCLA, USC, Illinois, and Michigan—he made the bold decision to head to the University of Michigan. Why? Because Michigan was known for producing NFL quarterbacks, and Tommy already had his eyes on the big prize. He was dreaming *way* bigger than a local college. "If you don't play to win, don't play at all," he said, and that philosophy guided his every move.

While football was the driving force behind his ambitions, life wasn't *only* scoring touchdowns for Tommy. Outside of the game, there was another side to him, one that made him just as unforgettable as his arm on the field. Beneath the competitiveness and big dreams, Tommy was also a bit of a class clown. He loved pulling pranks on his friends and cracking jokes to keep things light. His teachers said he was charming but not exactly a straight-A student. "He wasn't the smartest kid in the class," one of his old coaches joked, "but he was the smartest kid on the field." He also had a huge appetite, both for food and fun. His teammates remember how he could demolish a plate of food like it was his full-time job. One of his coaches said, "If Tommy attacked defenses the way he attacked spaghetti, he'd be unstoppable." Then there were his sisters. Remember those three older sisters who teased him endlessly as a kid? By the time Tommy hit high school, they were his biggest cheerleaders. Maureen, Julie, and Nancy would show up to his games, screaming louder than anyone else in the stands. "You've got this, Tommy!" they'd shout, embarrassing him half to death. But deep down, he loved it.

Back to the field, by his senior year, Tommy Brady was the undisputed star of the Serra football team. He had racked up 3,702 passing yards, 31 touchdowns, and enough awards to make a trophy case groan under the weight. He was named All-State, earned All-Far West honors, and was voted the team's Most Valuable Player. Not bad for a kid who started out on an 0–8 team, huh? Yet Tommy wasn't satisfied with high school glory. He wanted more. He wanted to test himself against the best players in the country. "You guys know how many times I've been turned down in my life?" he said. "To be told how many times that I couldn't accomplish something?" He wasn't going to let anyone—or anything—stand in the way of his dreams.

So, with his VHS tapes in the mail and a dream in his heart, Tommy Brady graduated from Junípero Serra High School in 1995 and packed his bags for Ann Arbor, Michigan. Indeed, he wasn't the the toughest or the most talked-about quarterback in the country, but he had something even better: the determination to prove everyone wrong. And boy, was the world in for a surprise.

When Tommy Brady arrived at the University of Michigan in 1995, it didn't feel like the start of something legendary. There were no cameras, no press, and definitely no confetti. What greeted him instead was a campus that seemed impossibly vast, a depth chart that had his name buried in the seventh spot at quarterback, and the kind of biting cold that made him wonder if his California blood could handle it. He stepped onto Ann Arbor's sprawling grounds with a duffel bag slung over one shoulder, clutching the dreams of a kid who hadn't yet been told that greatness wasn't supposed to be in his future. Michigan Stadium loomed in the distance, a giant coliseum promising glory to those who could survive the climb. The sea of maize and blue banners rippled in the breeze, and as Tommy scanned the endless brick buildings and winding paths, he cracked a joke to himself: "I'm gonna need a map just to find the cafeteria."

But he wasn't there for the cafeterias, and certainly not for the cold weather. Tom had one goal: to prove he belonged. And yet, as he walked into the Wolverines' first team meeting, his heart sank. Everywhere he looked, there were giants—guys who looked more like NFL players than students. He sat quietly at the back of the room, a lanky, wide-eyed freshman from California who was barely noticed. The head coach welcomed the team, announced the starting lineup, and began listing the quarterbacks in order. When Tom's name came dead last, his competitive fire kicked in. *Seventh string? We'll see about that.*

Tom didn't whine, and he definitely didn't quit. Instead, he showed up to every practice like it was a tryout. He stayed late, throwing passes to whoever was willing to catch them. When the starters went home, Tom stuck around, practicing footwork, working on timing, and soaking up advice from coaches and teammates like a sponge. It wasn't glamorous, and nobody was paying attention—yet. "You push your body to the limits," Tom would later say, "but you also train your mind to believe in the process."

But let's not sugarcoat it—those first few years were tough. Tom redshirted his freshman year, meaning he didn't play a single snap. During his second year, he managed to climb the depth chart slightly, earning a backup role. But his big moment came during a game against UCLA. The coach sent Tom in for his first series, and he jogged onto the field with a nervous energy he could feel in his fingertips. Ann Arbor's Michigan Stadium, affectionately called "The Big House," roared with over 100,000 fans. Tom lined up under center, took the snap, and fired his first college pass—a perfectly timed spiral, straight into the hands of... a UCLA defender. Pick-six.

Back on the sidelines, Tom clenched his jaw. There wasn't time to feel sorry for himself. He knew he'd get another chance, and when he did, he'd be ready. "You have to take the good with the bad," he later said about that moment. It became a defining trait of his career: never dwelling on mistakes, always focusing on the next play.

After three years of grinding it out, Tom finally earned the starting quarterback job for Michigan. But even then, nothing came easy. The coaching staff recruited Drew Henson, a five-star golden boy who was supposed to be the next big thing. For a while, the two quarterbacks alternated games, a frustrating situation for both of them. But Tom, as always, put his head down and went to work.

In his final season in 1999, Tom silenced the doubters. He led Michigan to comeback victories over Penn State and Ohio State, two of the team's biggest rivals. His performance in the Orange Bowl against Alabama became the stuff of college football legend: 369 passing yards, four touchdowns, and a game-winning overtime drive. The scouts were finally paying attention. One coach said, "Tom Brady might not look like much, but you can't measure his heart."

When the 2000 NFL Draft began, Tom sat in his family's living room in San Mateo, California, surrounded by his parents and three sisters. Galynn, his mom, had made snacks—chips, dip, cookies, the works—because that's what moms do when their kids are nervous. The Brady family tried to stay upbeat, cracking jokes to keep the mood light. But as round after round passed, and pick after pick came and went, the laughter faded.

Tom sat on the couch, hunched forward, staring at the TV. The names being called out were a parade of quarterbacks—Chad Pennington, Giovanni Carmazzi, Tee Martin—guys Tom knew he could outplay. His dad, Tom Sr., tried to keep spirits high, but even he was starting to look at the clock. Tom's sisters hovered nearby, biting their nails, unsure of what to say. By the fifth round, Tom couldn't take it anymore. He stood up, grabbed his keys, and said, "I'm going for a walk." He needed air, space, something to calm the storm brewing in his chest. Galynn called after him, "Tommy, don't go far! You'll miss the call!" Tom waved her off, thinking, *What call?*

And then, late in the sixth round of the 2000 NFL Draft, the phone finally rang. The Brady family's living room, once filled with laughter and small talk, had fallen silent hours ago. Galynn Brady had stopped pacing, her nervous energy replaced by quiet prayers as she sat clutching her husband's hand. Tom Sr. reached for the phone, his voice steady despite the electric tension in the air. "Hello?" On the other end was Bill Belichick's assistant.

"Mr. Brady? This is the New England Patriots. We've just selected Tom with the 199th pick."

Tom, still out on a walk to clear his head, walked back just as his dad hung up the phone. "Tommy," his dad called, his voice breaking slightly, "you're a Patriot." For a moment, there was stunned silence—and then the room exploded. His sisters screamed, Galynn hugged Tom so tightly he almost lost his breath, and even Tom Sr., the stoic rock of the family, wiped away a tear. Tom hugged everyone there, and then sat down on the couch. The cheers quieted, the moment settling into something deeper. Tom stared straight ahead, his jaw tight but his eyes full of fire saying: "I'm going to make them proud."

When Tom arrived at the Patriots' training facility, reality hit like a bucket of cold water. He wasn't walking into the spotlight; he was walking into a storm of indifference. The Patriots staff barely looked at him—he was a sixth-round pick, after all, the kind of guy most teams draft as an afterthought. In the locker room, his jersey hung on a corner peg, far from the rows of starters. If this was his shot, it wasn't going to be handed to him.

At his very first team meeting, he shook hands with Robert Kraft, the team's owner, and introduced himself with a line that would later become legendary: "Hi, I'm Tom Brady, and I'm the best decision this organization has ever made." Bold? Sure. But to Tom, it was just truth waiting to be proven. The rookie threw himself into every drill, every practice, like a man with everything to prove. When the starters headed to the locker room, Tom stayed behind, throwing extra passes to anyone who would catch them. Every rep felt like an audition for his dream. By the end of his rookie season, he had clawed his way up the depth chart to become Drew Bledsoe's backup. It wasn't glamorous, but it was progress.

And then, in Week 2 of the 2001 season, everything changed. The Patriots were facing the Jets when Drew Bledsoe took a devastating hit that left him with internal injuries. The stadium held its breath as trainers rushed to the field, and when the huddle broke, it wasn't Bledsoe walking back out. It was Tom Brady.

He jogged onto the field with a calmness that seemed to defy the moment. The fans didn't know him, the announcers barely mentioned him, but Tom's teammates noticed something immediately: the kid wasn't nervous. He was ready. Over the next few weeks, Tom led the Patriots to an 11–3 record in games he started. Slowly but surely, the backup quarterback nobody had cared about became the guy everyone was talking about.

The playoffs came, and with them, one of the most controversial games in NFL history: *The Tuck Rule Game.* Played in a snowstorm so thick it looked like the field had been dropped in the middle of a snow globe, the Patriots faced the Raiders in the AFC Divisional Round. Late in the game, with New England trailing, Tom dropped back to pass and was hit from behind. The ball popped loose, and Oakland recovered. Game over—or so it seemed. But after reviewing the play, the officials ruled it an incomplete pass thanks to the obscure "tuck rule," giving the Patriots another chance. They won in overtime, and Tom Brady became an instant hero.

Two weeks later, on the grandest stage in sports, under the blinding lights of Super Bowl XXXVI, Tom Brady's legend was forged. The Patriots were up against the "Greatest Show on Turf," the St. Louis Rams, a team so dominant they seemed untouchable, but there was Tom, just 24 years old, standing on the sideline as the game sat tied 17–17, approaching the end. The pressure in the stadium was suffocating—fans screamed, and the weight of the moment pressed down like a mountain. When Tom jogged onto the field, there was no panic in his eyes. His teammates would later say, "He looked like he'd done it a hundred times before." The drive started deep in Patriots territory, and every snap was a gamble. Tom dropped back again and again, scanning the field with the calm precision of a surgeon. He wasn't thinking about the odds, the doubters, or the magnitude of the moment—he was locked in. A quick out here. A dart over the middle there. The chains moved. The clock ticked. The Rams' defenders swarmed him like wolves on every play, but Tom stood tall, unshaken. "He's got ice in his veins," a commentator marveled as Brady marched his team closer to field goal range. And then came the kick. The Patriots lined up for a 48-yard field goal attempt as the final seconds drained off the clock. Tom stood on the sideline, his helmet tucked under his arm, staring at the field with such intensity, as if he knew his life was about to change. Adam Vinatieri's foot met the ball, sending it arcing through the air. The crowd held its collective breath. Then—*boom*, it sailed through the uprights. The stadium erupted in chaos. The Patriots had done the unthinkable: a 20–17 victory over one of the greatest teams in NFL history. In the confetti-strewn aftermath, Tom stood surrounded by cameras, the Lombardi Trophy glinting in his hands, his teammates chanting his name. He was named Super Bowl MVP, but it was bigger than that. He wasn't just a kid from San Mateo anymore. The sixth-round afterthought had arrived, and the NFL would never be the same.

The next 20 years unfolded like the kind of fairy tale that kids dream about but never believe in. Tom Brady became a game-changer who turned impossible dreams into reality. He led the Patriots to six more Super Bowl victories, shattered records that once seemed untouchable, and silenced every critic who had doubted him along the way. There were moments that etched themselves into football history: the perfect 2007 season (though heartbreakingly spoiled by the Giants in the Super Bowl), the jaw-dropping 28–3 comeback against the Falcons in Super Bowl LI, and the triumphant late-career renaissance with the Tampa Bay Buccaneers, where he won his seventh Super Bowl at age 43.

The way Tom carried himself was also remarkable. He led with a quiet, unshakable confidence that inspired his teammates to believe they could win no matter the odds. "When you're one of the leaders of the team, there are no days off," Tom often said, and he lived those words every single day.

When Tom Brady retired in 2023, his jaw-dropping numbers—89,214 passing yards, 649 touchdowns, and seven Super Bowl rings—were just part of the story. What really stands out is how he never let setbacks define him and always found a way to keep going, no matter what. Even now, his days are anything but quiet—breaking down plays, building new projects, or just tossing a football with his kids. His journey is a powerful reminder: big dreams take hard work, and every challenge is a chance to grow stronger. As Tom once said, "I didn't come this far to only come this far." And maybe that's the biggest takeaway—there's always more to aim for, as long as you're willing to keep trying.

Peyton Manning

THE PLAY-CALLING PRODIGY

Peyton Manning's story starts in a house where football and family were as inseparable as peanut butter and jelly. He is born in New Orleans, Louisiana, in 1976. He's the middle child, squished between an older brother, Cooper, and a younger brother, Eli, in a family so connected to football they're practically royalty—the "Manning Dynasty" people call them. His dad, Archie Manning, is a big name in the National Football League, known mostly for his time as quarterback of the New Orleans Saints. But the funny thing is, Archie doesn't push his kids into football. He lets them mess around with whatever sports they want. Basketball, baseball, and of course, football fill the Manning backyard with shouting, laughter, and the occasional crash that probably sends Mrs. Manning running to check for broken bones.

Peyton grows up idolizing his dad, but not in a "must-follow-in-dad's-footsteps" kind of way. He's got this easygoing family vibe where, even though they're living in the shadow of a famous quarterback, life is pretty normal. Archie teaches his boys about football without pressure. He's out there tossing passes with them, sure, but he's also sharing deeper stuff—like teamwork, staying humble, and not giving up just because you drop the ball once or twice (or fifty times). Peyton says, "I think my love for football comes from the things my dad taught me." It's not just about throwing a ball; it's about doing things right, working hard, and having fun.

Then there's Cooper, Peyton's older brother, who's like his own personal coach-slash-comedian. Cooper's the big brother who knows how to catch every pass Peyton throws and is funny enough to keep Peyton laughing even when things get serious. In high school, Cooper becomes an All-State wide receiver, snagging Peyton's passes like he's got magnets for hands. They are unstoppable—Cooper out there, a blur in green and white, with Peyton launching passes like mini-cannonballs. They're practically telepathic on the field, setting each other up for jaw-dropping plays that leave the crowd buzzing. But then, right before Cooper heads to college, doctors diagnose him with a condition that ends his football dreams instantly. Peyton is crushed, watching his hero and big brother go from a rising football star to someone who has to give up the game for good. Cooper stays strong, though, shifting his focus to business and starting a family, becoming a huge inspiration for Peyton. Even as adults, Peyton says, "Cooper is the funniest guy I know. I always try to make him proud."

In high school at Isidore Newman School, Peyton dives head-first into football. He becomes a starter and racks up stats like nobody's business—over 7,000 passing yards and 92 touchdowns! His record as a starter is an incredible 34 wins to just 5 losses. Coaches and scouts across the country are already whispering about the "next Manning," but at school, Peyton's still "that lanky kid who can't stop memorizing weird stuff." Seriously, the guy has a memory like a supercomputer. He's not only remembering playbooks and routes, he's memorizing old Motown songs on road trips. One of his friends, Justin, recalls a time when they're driving to some game, and Peyton, only 11 or 12, is sitting in the back seat naming every song and artist that plays on the radio. Reyna's parents are just staring at him, like, "What kind of kid knows this much about music from thirty years ago?"

And Peyton doesn't stop there. He's obsessed with every little detail about football, even the games he never watches. His friend Thad Teaford once says, "Peyton knew every single player his dad played with. He could tell you exactly what the next play would be, who caught every touchdown, and where each guy was from. It was like the light switch was on from the second he was born." In fact, his bedroom wall is practically a spider web of sticky notes and ideas. One of his high school buddies, Nate Stibbs, remembers walking into Peyton's room and seeing about 250 sticky notes all over the walls. "If he had an idea, he'd write it down on a yellow sticky note and slap it up there," Stibbs says, shaking his head. It's like a mini detective board straight out of a crime show, but instead of clues to catch a criminal, it's packed with things like practice strategies, homework reminders, and random stuff Peyton doesn't want to forget.

Sometimes Peyton's focus on winning gets him into trouble. Like this one time, he's on a "bitty basketball" team in elementary school, and one of the neighborhood dads is the coach. This guy isn't exactly a basketball expert; he's more like, "Hey kids, let's go out there and have fun!" That does *not* sit well with young Peyton. After they lose a game, the coach gives a typical "we'll-get-'em-next-time" speech, trying to keep things light, but Peyton has had enough. He stands up, points his finger, and says, "No, the reason we lost is because you don't know what you're doing as a coach." Yikes. Later, Archie drags Peyton over to the coach's house to apologize, and Peyton is bawling the whole way, thinking his dad might actually make him quit the team. "It was a good lesson on keeping my mouth shut," Peyton admits, probably wincing at the memory.

When he's not busy critiquing his coaches, Peyton's also stirring up all kinds of mischief. He and his friends love pulling pranks. They prank call people *before* the days of Caller ID, pretending to be reporters calling parents of high school athletes. His friend Baldwin Montgomery says, "We'd call someone's dad and pretend we were from Blue Chip magazine, asking about their son's stats. The dads ate it up! We'd ask ridiculous stuff, like 'Does he wear a neck roll? How much can he bench?' We got some crazy answers." It works great until Peyton leaves a voicemail for one dad who recognizes his voice, and of course, Archie gets a call. Peyton has to make yet another round of apologies.

But Peyton also knows when to turn the funny business off and get serious. He's got this relentless work ethic that sets him apart. He isn't naturally fast, and in eighth grade, he barely lifts the bar in the weight room. "We did a speed camp with the track coach, and Peyton was running with the heaviest kid there," Teaford says. "But by senior year, he's running a respectable 40-yard dash and lifting like a beast." Peyton keeps getting stronger because he practices constantly. His receivers at Newman High School remember him making them run the same five-yard out route over and over. Tight end Mike Keck says, "I didn't get it. I thought, 'Why can't we do a more exciting route?' But Peyton knew how important timing was. He wanted that ball there the instant I turned my head." Peyton's motto might as well be "out-prepare everyone," and his friends see that determination in him long before the NFL scouts do.

On the baseball team, he's known for playing pranks as well, like swapping towels with his friends so they end up with tiny washcloths instead of full-sized towels. One time, he hands his friend Stibbs a washcloth as a joke, but things backfire when the team loses their game and the coach ends up with the washcloth instead. The coach storms out of the showers, furious, demanding to know who's responsible. Stibbs looks over at Peyton, who's hunched down, not daring to look up. "You almost got us killed with that prank," Stibbs mutters, but they laugh about it for years.

So by the time Peyton's senior year rolls around, he's not only the top quarterback recruit in the country, he's also one of the most respected kids in school. He's got this knack for bringing people together, whether it's through his dedication on the field or his goofy antics off of it. The guy has a memory for everything—plays, songs, people's names—and he's already a leader, even if he still sometimes acts like a big kid. Peyton's friends, coaches, and family know he's headed somewhere special. Even if he takes a different path than everyone expects, you get the feeling he's going to leave a mark wherever he goes.

As high school wraps up, Peyton Manning faces a decision that the whole football world has been buzzing about: where will he play college ball? His father, Archie, played at the University of Mississippi, a school so tied to the Manning family that people practically expect Peyton to walk onto campus in an Ole Miss jersey with "MANNING" already printed on the back. His brother Cooper had planned to go there too, before his condition forced him to give up football. It's like Ole Miss is part of the family DNA, and the whole world assumes Peyton's heading that way. But Peyton isn't one to let others decide his path. He loves Ole Miss, sure, but he wants a place that feels like his own, somewhere he can write his own story.

So when he chooses the University of Tennessee, a rival school, it's like dropping a firecracker in the middle of SEC fandom. Ole Miss fans practically howl in disbelief, Tennessee fans throw up their arms in victory, and the media goes wild. It's a bold move, one that instantly makes him a target for extra scrutiny and maybe a few dirty looks from hardcore Ole Miss folks. But that's Peyton—always willing to take the harder road if it means he can do things his way. He says later, "I had to make my own path. My dad respected that. I wanted a challenge." And Tennessee, with its massive crowds, its powerhouse football program, and its sea of orange jerseys, is definitely going to give him one.

The day Peyton steps onto the campus at Tennessee, he's a freshman with a goofy grin, a mop of curly hair, and a determination that's practically radiating off him like heat. At first, he's third string—yep, third in line for the quarterback spot. Most people would see that as a chance to relax, to coast a little before stepping up, but not Peyton. He dives into the Tennessee playbook like it's the most thrilling novel he's ever read, memorizing formations and routes until he's practically reciting them in his sleep. He's also picking up tips from the starting QB, Todd Helton, who just so happens to be a future Major League Baseball player (because Peyton's life is full of casual connections to greatness). But when Helton and the second-string quarterback both get injured early in the season, Peyton finally gets his shot. He steps onto the field with that trademark Manning focus, and once he starts, he never looks back.

Now, you have to understand, college football in Tennessee isn't just a sport—it's more like a weekly statewide holiday. On Saturdays, Neyland Stadium in Knoxville fills up with over 100,000 fans, a sea of orange stretching as far as the eye can see. People come from all over, some of them driving hours to be part of the spectacle. And Peyton, who's still barely out of high school, stands at the center of it all, like a young general leading an army. As the season goes on, he gets more and more comfortable, turning into a leader for the Volunteers with the same ease that he turned his high school buddies into a tight-knit team. Pretty soon, he's throwing touchdowns left and right, racking up yards, and making college defenses look like they're playing in slow motion.

By his junior year, Peyton Manning is a college football legend in the making. He leads Tennessee to one victory after another, packing his stat sheet with thousands of passing yards and enough touchdowns to make other quarterbacks jealous. His stats are so good that NFL scouts start practically camping outside his dorm, whispering about draft positions and signing bonuses. But Peyton has his own plans. He's earned enough credits to graduate early, and everyone assumes he'll declare for the NFL draft. Most players in his position would jump at the chance. But Peyton? He surprises everyone by choosing to stay for his senior year. "I wanted one more season with my teammates," he says. "One more chance to play for Tennessee, to give it everything." It's classic Peyton, valuing friendships and loyalty over the easy money waiting for him in the pros.

Staying another year isn't just about football for Peyton, though. He's living off-campus now, in a house with some of his closest friends, getting a taste of what life is like beyond the strict schedule of a college athlete. He's famous, sure, but around his friends, he's still just Peyton—the guy who remembers the lyrics to every Motown song, the prankster who once left a sticky note trail down the entire hallway just to mess with his roommates, the guy who'll sit in the student section at basketball games and cheer until he's hoarse. He's still got that same down-to-earth charm that keeps him close to his high school friends back home, and even with his busy schedule, he's making sure those friendships don't fade. "I really value those friendships," Peyton says. "They're the guys who knew me before all this. They keep me grounded."

As Peyton's senior year approaches, anticipation surges through the campus like electricity. He's no longer just Tennessee's star quarterback; he's become a legend in the making, someone who brings intensity and inspiration with every snap. The team, the fans, everyone feels it—this final season is building up to something incredible, something unforgettable.

And when his senior year finally begins, Peyton storms onto the field like a man on a mission. He throws for a jaw-dropping 3,819 yards and 36 touchdowns, capping off his college career with stats that send fans into a frenzy, coaches breathing sighs of relief, and defenses desperately trying to keep up. His leadership shines as bright as his arm; he's out there rallying teammates, shouting out defensive shifts before the snap, making split-second adjustments that leave opponents scrambling. You can see it in the eyes of the other teams—they know he's a step ahead, thinking three moves in advance like a chess master. Peyton's magic got this connection with the fans that's as real as it gets—signing autographs, shaking hands, chatting with anyone who wants a moment of his time. It's no wonder Tennessee adores him and why they start calling him "the Sheriff." He owns the field with a no-nonsense authority that makes everyone feel they're in safe hands.

The accolades start pouring in. He's named an All-American, wins the prestigious Sullivan Award (given to the top college athlete in the country), and graduates Phi Beta Kappa with a degree in speech communications. But what really sticks with people is his decision to put off the NFL for that final year, showing that he isn't all about fame and fortune. He's there for his team, for his friends, and for Tennessee. One of his professors even says Peyton could go into politics or public speaking if football doesn't work out, and you can almost see it—Peyton Manning, governor of Tennessee, shaking hands and cracking jokes at town hall meetings.

The respect Peyton earns at Tennessee goes way beyond the football field. His name becomes a kind of legend around campus. There's even a road near the stadium called "Peyton Manning Pass," as if the university itself wants to tip its hat to the guy who brought so much pride to their school. Students wear his jersey, young quarterbacks try to mimic his stance, and fans talk about his games like they're passing down family stories. By the time he graduates, it's clear that Peyton Manning is a part of Tennessee history. Years later, people still tell stories about his time there, about how he made them believe anything was possible on a Saturday afternoon in Knoxville.

And as he finishes up that final season, everyone knows he's ready for the NFL. The scouts are practically salivating over his numbers, his leadership, his work ethic. Peyton, though, keeps things in perspective. He's grateful for the friends he's made, the coaches who've shaped him, and the fans who've cheered him on. He says goodbye to the University of Tennessee with a heart full of gratitude and a promise to come back, whether it's for a reunion game or to watch from the stands. But for now, he's got bigger stages waiting for him, bigger challenges to tackle. And as he steps away from college life, he's carrying with him everything he's learned—not just about football, but about loyalty, hard work, and making the most of every moment.

Finally, the big day arrives: April 18, 1998. The Indianapolis Colts pick Peyton Manning as the number one player in the NFL Draft. Choosing between Peyton and Ryan Leaf, another top guy, caused so much fuss you'd think people were picking a superhero! But when Peyton gets the call, he's all set. He shows up in Indy with that famous Manning smile and a plan already cooking in his head. On his first flight to Indianapolis, he learns the names of every single person working in the Colts' office. That's just Peyton being Peyton—the kid who had sticky notes all over his bedroom walls, now ready to learn a whole playbook (and maybe the phone book too) before he even high-fives his new teammates.

But guess what? The NFL isn't about to throw him a party. In his first season, Peyton faces the tough world of pro football. He throws 28 interceptions that year—a rookie record! Yikes! But instead of getting upset, Peyton sees it as a challenge. After every bad game, every interception, he's back watching game films, figuring out what went wrong and how to fix it. His coach, Jim Mora, sometimes finds Peyton staying so late at practice that the janitor hands him the keys and says, "Don't forget to turn off the lights!" Peyton just shrugs and says, "I just want to make sure I'm doing everything I can." That hard work—the kind that goes the extra mile—quickly earns him respect from his coaches, teammates, and fans.

All that hard work pays off! In his second season, Peyton leads the Colts to a 13-3 record—a huge change from their rookie troubles. Suddenly, Indianapolis—a place better known for basketball—is cheering like crazy on Sundays. Colts fans start showing up in big numbers, filling the RCA Dome to watch their young quarterback work his magic. Peyton doesn't just throw the ball; he runs the show! He shouts out instructions, changes plays on the spot, and points at defenders like he's playing "Simon Says." That's why they call him "The Sheriff." He's the guy who rides into town, cleans up the mess, and leaves things better than he found them.

And the fans? Oh, they're crazy about him! Indianapolis turns into a football town almost overnight, with Peyton as the hero. Kids start wearing No. 18 jerseys, families gather around TVs to watch his games, and the whole city holds its breath every time he steps on the field. Peyton feels the love and gives it right back, signing autographs, visiting schools, and chatting with fans like they're old buddies. He even starts the PeyBack Foundation in 1999, a charity to help kids who need it in Indiana, Tennessee, and Louisiana. The foundation brings thousands of kids to Colts games, holiday dinners, and other fun events all year long. Peyton's out there shaking hands, posing for pictures, and making kids feel like they're the real MVPs—even though they don't have to throw a single touchdown!

But even with all the regular-season magic, the playoffs turn into Peyton's own "unlucky streak." The Colts run into trouble, often thanks to their rivals, the New England Patriots, led by quarterback Tom Brady. The Brady-Manning rivalry is legendary, and for years, Brady seems to come out on top. In the 2003 AFC Championship, Peyton throws four interceptions, and the Colts lose 24-14. Ouch again! The next year, the Patriots beat them again, 20-3. It's like trying to reach the cookie jar on the top shelf—so close yet so far! But Peyton doesn't give up. Instead, he tries even harder, pushing himself and his teammates to work like never before. He wins two NFL MVP awards in a row in 2003 and 2004, showing he's one of the best, but the Super Bowl still feels just out of reach.

At last, in the 2006 season, everything falls into place. Peyton and the Colts charge through the playoffs, beating—you guessed it—the Patriots in an epic AFC Championship Game. Down 21-3 in the first half, the Colts make an amazing comeback, with Peyton throwing for 349 yards and leading the team to a 38-34 victory. The stadium goes wild! Colts fans are losing their minds, high-fiving strangers, crying, and shouting "Peyton! Peyton!" It's the win they've been dreaming of, and it takes them straight to Super Bowl XLI. There, on a rainy night in Miami, Peyton finally gets his crown, leading the Colts to a 29-17 victory over the Chicago Bears. He's named Super Bowl MVP, standing tall with confetti raining down, his smile bigger than ever. He smiles so big you'd think he just found out pizza is a vegetable! Indianapolis has its championship, and Peyton Manning has made his mark in history.

But if you think Peyton kicks back after that, think again! He keeps breaking records like they're piñatas at a birthday party, putting up numbers that change what it means to be a quarterback. In 2009, he wins his fourth MVP award—more than any player ever! By now, he's broken Dan Marino's single-season touchdown record, thrown for over 12,000 yards in his first three seasons, and set countless records for passes, touchdowns, and yards. It's like there's nothing Peyton can't do! He breaks records like most people break pencils! Colts fans start talking about him like a legend. They even put up a statue of him outside Lucas Oil Stadium, honoring the man who made Indianapolis a football town.

But then, in 2011, Peyton hits a big bump in the road. A neck injury keeps him out for the whole season, and the Colts, having a tough year without him, decide to let him go. After

14 seasons, Peyton leaves Indianapolis. It's a tearful goodbye. Fans cry, Peyton thanks the city, and for a moment, it feels like the end of an era. But Peyton isn't finished—not even close! In true comeback fashion, he signs with the Denver Broncos in 2012, ready to show he still has lots of football left in him. He switches teams faster than you can say "Omaha!"

After parting ways with Indianapolis, Peyton begins a new chapter in 2012 with the Denver Broncos, and wow, does he bring it! He picks up right where he left off, tossing touchdown after touchdown and leading the Broncos to the playoffs again and again. In 2013, he has what might be his best season ever, setting NFL records for passing yards (5,477) and touchdowns (55). He throws touchdowns like kids throw confetti at a birthday party! He's unstoppable, winning his fifth MVP award and making football look like a walk in the park. His old Colts teammates joke that Peyton must be part robot, but really, it's all hard work. He's still the same guy who covered his bedroom walls with sticky notes and studied playbooks like bedtime stories.

In 2016, Peyton makes it to the Super Bowl again, this time with the Broncos. It's Super Bowl 50, and at 39 years old, Peyton leads his team to victory over the heavily favored Carolina Panthers. With this win, he becomes the first quarterback to win Super Bowls with two different teams—a feat that puts him in the history books again! As the confetti falls, Peyton takes it all in, enjoying what he knows will be his probably last game. Soon after, as the world awaits with bated breath, he announces what everyone suspected: this was indeed his final game. He steps away from football as a champion, with a legacy that will inspire generations to come.

He retires on top—like finishing a video game on the hardest level without losing a life! Even after he stops playing, Peyton's big personality keeps him close to fans' hearts. He shows up in commercials, makes guest appearances on "Saturday Night Live" (where he hilariously coaches kids in a fake ad, tossing footballs at them like they're pro players), and even hosts his own show on ESPN+, called "Peyton's Places." On the show, he travels around, interviews other football legends, shares laughs, and nerds out over the history of the game he loves. In true Peyton style, he does it with humor and hard work, making people laugh one minute and sharing awesome football facts the next. "I just love the game," he says. "And I love talking about it." He coaches kids on TV—probably because he missed firing footballs at people!

Then there's the Manningcast, a different kind of Monday Night Football show that Peyton co-hosts with his brother Eli. The two of them sit in their living rooms, watching games while cracking jokes, telling stories, and bringing on guest stars from all over sports and entertainment. It's like watching football with your funniest friends—except these friends are superstar quarterbacks! It's hilarious and unpredictable, with Peyton and Eli bouncing off each other like the funniest duo in the NFL. Fans tune in for the laughs but stay for the cool insights, because Peyton's football brain is as sharp as ever, calling plays and reading defenses like he's still on the field.

Peyton Manning's life is a tale of hard work, family, and a love for the game that never fades. He's a legend, a goofball, a prankster, a leader, and most of all, a guy who stays true to his roots. Whether he's running the Manning Passing Academy with his dad and brothers, giving millions through his PeyBack Foundation, or joking with his friends about old high school pranks, he holds onto the values he learned growing up. He might have the trophies, but he still remembers how to have fun—like when he pranked his buddies by filling their lockers with popcorn! And that's what makes Peyton Manning unforgettable—he's still the same guy who remembers every friend, every fan, and every little moment that got him here.

Larry Fitzgerald

The Unstoppable Wide Receiver

Larry Fitzgerald Jr. arrived on a crisp August 31, 1983, in the lively city of Minneapolis, Minnesota—a place where winters are so cold, even penguins would shiver! But don't worry, the people there have hearts warmer than a toasted marshmallow. There, Larry's path to becoming a football superstar didn't start with fireworks, it began quietly, way before he was catching touchdowns or setting NFL records. Born into a regular family where hard work was expected just like saying "Bless you" after a sneeze, and then, Larry didn't see football as his destiny just yet.

His dad, Larry Sr., was a sportswriter. Imagine having a dad who gets to chat with famous athletes all the time! For young Larry, his dad's job was like having a backstage pass to a superhero movie. "Wait, you talked to who?!" he'd probably say with wide eyes. His fascination with sports started bubbling up like a fizzy soda.

Larry Jr.'s mom, Carol, was the glue of the family. She was the kind of mom who'd remind you to mind your manners, like saying "please" and "thank you" was as important as remembering your own name. Carol thought football was just a fun thing to do on weekends—she worried about her boys getting hurt. Larry Sr. agreed, thinking football could be too rough. He even tried to keep Larry Jr. from playing tackle football for as long as possible. But let's face it, Larry had more energy than a puppy on a sugar rush!

When Larry was about ten, Carol pulled a pretty sneaky move. She went ahead and signed him up for pee wee football behind his dad's back! The first time Larry put on that too-big helmet, he looked like a bobblehead, but hey, could he play! He was like a tiny tornado on the field, leaving everyone wondering, "Who's that kid, and did he just have three bowls of lightning for breakfast?" His dad, swept up in the rush of it all, had to admit, "Larry was always full of energy and loved to compete. From the time he was born, he had sports in his sights." If there was a game to be played, Larry was there, grinning like he just found the last cookie in the jar.

At that time, when Larry wasn't tossing a ball, he was working. His family owned a couple of grocery stores, and his parents believed in teaching their sons the value of hard work. They didn't want Larry and his younger brother, Marcus, to grow up thinking the world was made of cotton candy and rainbows. So, when they weren't in school, the boys had jobs at the family store. Larry stocked shelves, rang up customers, and swept floors—though we're pretty sure he wished the broom was a football. It wasn't the most exciting job for a kid who'd rather be zooming around outside, but it taught him grit. He learned that to get what he wanted, he'd have to work hard, stay focused, and finish the job—even when he'd rather be doing just about anything else. This lesson stuck with him, from the pee wee fields all the way to the NFL.

As Larry grew up, life started testing him, he struggled in school, especially when it came to paying attention in class. His parents noticed he was having trouble concentrating—maybe his brain was doing touchdown dances when it should've been solving math problems! They made a tough decision to pull him out of his regular school and send him to Pilgrim Lutheran, a smaller private school where they hoped he'd get the help he needed. The change was good, and Larry started finding his groove with schoolwork, but it was still a bit like trying to catch a slippery fish.

When he got to high school at Minnehaha Academy, he played both basketball and football. It was there that he started to glimpse what he might be capable of—at least on the field. High school football was a whole new ball game, and Larry was ready to give it everything he had. But life threw him a curveball. When he was just a freshman, his mom, Carol, got really sick. The news caught him by surprise. Suddenly, football and school didn't seem so important. All he could think about was his mom and the scary thought that she might not be there to cheer him on. Watching her go through surgeries and treatments was tough—tougher than any opponent he'd face on the field. But Carol was as strong as a superhero, fighting with everything she had. Larry drew strength from her courage. It was a hard lesson in toughness, but one he'd never forget.

During these years, Larry's world was all about football, family, and—you guessed it—more football. His dad would take him and Marcus to practices and games, giving them a taste of the sport without diving into the deep end just yet. By the time Larry was 14 or 15, he scored a gig as a ball boy for the Minnesota Vikings, thanks to his dad's connections. Imagine this: one minute, Larry was just a regular kid watching football on TV; the next, he was standing right there on the sidelines, handing balls to his heroes! "Coach Green gave me the opportunity of a lifetime," Larry said, his voice filled with awe even years later. "I got to be around my childhood idols—Cris Carter, Warren Moon, Joey Browner, Randy Moss, and Robert Smith." For him, it was like stepping into a real-life video game, with every practice and game an adventure where he wasn't just a fan anymore—he was part of the action, learning from legends up close.

But even dream jobs have rules. One night, Larry stayed out past curfew during camp, and security reported it to his dad. Uh-oh! Larry Sr. wasn't thrilled. Feeling embarrassed, he pulled Larry off the job to teach him a lesson, reminding him that with great power comes great responsibility—or at least, that you should be home on time! Larry sweated it out for a while, but eventually, his dad let him return. He learned that if he wanted to be around greatness, he had to act the part.

Soon enough, Larry was on every high school scout's radar, a name that couldn't be ignored. He transferred to the Academy of Holy Angels, and that's where his game exploded. As a wide receiver, he was fast, fearless, and unstoppable. His team was strong—but Larry? He was a game-changer. By senior year, his talent was undeniable. College scouts swarmed like trick-or-treaters on Halloween, all hoping to reel in the brand new rising star. Nebraska, Ohio State, Michigan State, Penn State—they all lined up, ready to offer him a future. But Larry felt the magnetic pull to the University of Pittsburgh, where Coach Walt Harris promised him a chance to shine like never before. Yet, there was one teeny-tiny problem: his grades. When his mom was sick, school took a backseat, and now it was holding him back. His GPA wasn't high enough to get into Pittsburgh straight away. So, his family made another tough call. Larry would spend a year at Valley Forge Military Academy in Pennsylvania. Military school? For Larry, it sounded about as fun as eating broccoli-flavored ice cream! You guessed it—he wasn't really thrilled about it!

But his family believed it was what he needed, and he didn't have much of a choice—so off he went, leaving Minneapolis behind. At Valley Forge, he found himself in a world of strict routines and high expectations. The military structure wasn't easy—think early mornings, crisp uniforms, and lots of "Yes, sir!" At first, Larry felt out of place, like he was living in a totally different world. But slowly, the discipline started to sink in. It pushed him to be tougher, sharper, and more focused than ever before. By the end of the year, Larry had thrived, graduating with honors and feeling more prepared than ever to tackle his future at Pittsburgh.

Before he left for college, his family told him something he'd always known deep down: they believed in him. His dad said, "We told Larry we loved him and believed that he could do it." And with that, Larry set off on the next part of his journey, his bags packed with discipline, determination, and maybe a few snacks for the road. He was ready to chase his dreams—all the way to the NFL!

When Larry Fitzgerald finally set foot at the University of Pittsburgh, he felt like a rocket ready to launch! He wasn't just any new player with big dreams; he was a kid who had climbed mountains to get there (okay, maybe not real ones). Military school had toughened him up in ways he couldn't have imagined—think of it like superhero training camp. Now, he was more focused than ever. He was here to play football, to shine bright like a disco ball, and nothing less would do.

From the get-go, he was a nightmare for any player trying to cover him on the field. Larry was like a cheetah on roller skates! He had this incredible grip on the ball—once he caught it, it stays. In his freshman season in 2002, Larry burst onto the scene like a firecracker. In his second game against Texas A&M, he grabbed ten receptions for 103 yards. Not too shabby for a newbie!

As the season rolled on, Larry started stacking up stats like a kid collecting trading cards. Fans were beginning to whisper, "Who is this guy?" There was one game that really got people talking: November 2 against the super-strong Virginia Tech. Larry snagged five receptions for 105 yards and scored three touchdowns, helping Pitt win a tight game, 28–21. It was the kind of performance that made everyone sit up and say, "Whoa!"

By the end of his freshman year, Larry led the Big East Conference with 69 catches for 1,005 yards and twelve touchdowns. Not bad for a first-year player who probably still got lost finding his classrooms! Pitt made it to the Insight Bowl, and Larry showed up big time, snagging five receptions for 88 yards and a touchdown in a 38–13 win over Oregon State. His coach, Walt Harris, would say, "I remember thinking, man, this kid isn't playing like a freshman. He's playing like he's been here for years." Larry had this cool confidence, like he knew exactly where he was headed.

But 2002 was just the appetizer. In 2003, during his sophomore season, Larry went from being a rising star to a full-blown supernova! In the first game against Kent State, he immediately set the tone: six catches, 123 yards, and three touchdowns. It was like he was saying, "Buckle up, folks. It's showtime!" And showtime it was. Game after game, he left defenses scratching their heads, wondering if he had rocket boosters in his cleats.

Larry was playing chess while everyone else was playing checkers. He wasn't just running around; he was studying the defense, figuring out how to outsmart them. "If it's important to me, I usually remember it," he said later. And football? Super important! His brain was like a sponge, soaking up every play, every strategy.

But there was more fueling Larry than just a love for the game. His mom, Carol, was back home battling Illness again. The news hit him like a ton of bricks wrapped in sadness. He was heartbroken, but turned that pain into purpose. Every touchdown, every catch, was for her. It was his way of fighting alongside her. His dad noticed the change, saying, "I could tell something changed in Larry when he thought his mom might not get better." Larry played like every game was the championship, and in a way, it was. He put all his energy into sports, playing as if each game could help him feel a little stronger inside.

He broke records left and right. He had a streak of 18 consecutive games with a touchdown catch, breaking an NCAA record. By the end of the 2003 season, he had 92 catches for 1,672 yards and an eye-popping 22 touchdowns, leading the entire NCAA that year. His amazing performances earned him the 2003 Walter Camp Award, the Biletnikoff Award, and unanimous All-American honors. He was even a finalist for the Heisman Trophy, finishing second. Not too shabby for a kid who once thought military school sounded like a bad joke!

After that season, Larry felt it deep down—it was time. He was ready to tackle the NFL, the big leagues, the place where legends are made! Sure, on paper, he was still a sophomore, but in his heart? He was primed, focused, and fired up. Normally, players had to be three years out of high school to even think about the NFL draft. But Larry's path was anything but typical; it twisted and turned like a roller coaster zooming at top speed. See, he'd spent a year at Valley Forge Military Academy, a detour that ended up paving the way for a special exemption. And guess what? The NFL granted him that golden ticket!

But getting that "yes" was no easy feat. Larry's dad jumped in, helping him tackle stacks of paperwork, late-night calls, and all the little details. "We had to work with the NFL and show them that even though Larry was a sophomore, he'd have graduated with his high school class," his dad explained, smiling with pride. It took effort, teamwork, and, well, a whole lot of patience—talk about jumping through hoops! But in the end, Larry was set, his path to the NFL wide open, and the dream within reach.

Draft day came, and instead of going to the big event in New York, the Fitzgerald family decided to stay in Chicago for a more personal celebration. Both of Larry's grandfathers weren't feeling well, and they wanted to share this moment together as a family. They gathered at a hotel, hearts pounding like drums. Finally, with the third overall pick in the 2004 NFL Draft, the Arizona Cardinals selected Larry. The room exploded with cheers! Larry could hardly believe it. Yes! The kid from Minneapolis was heading to the NFL!

Larry's dad paused, letting the moment sink in like the warmth of a sunset after a long day. He looked back on all the grit, the sacrifices, the countless late-night talks—they'd walked this journey together, every step. And now, seeing Larry standing on the brink of the NFL, his heart swelled with pride—not just because Larry had made it, but because of the young man he'd become. Larry had stayed grounded, humble, and true to himself, even with the bright lights ahead. "I'm proud that our son trusted me and his mom," Larry Sr. shared, his voice filled with both pride and a touch of emotion. "He listened, he stayed on course, he did everything we asked." He could almost hear his late wife's voice, sharing in this proud, joyful moment.

With his family's love and support, Larry headed off to Arizona, ready to start the next chapter of his amazing journey. He put on the Cardinals' red and white jersey, feeling like a superhero donning his cape. As he stepped onto the field for his first professional game, he looked out at the roaring crowd and thought, "This is just the beginning." The kid from Minneapolis had arrived, and the NFL was about to see what he could do!

The Arizona desert greeted Larry Fitzgerald in 2004 with sunshine so bright, he probably needed extra-dark sunglasses! Stepping into the NFL, he was a rookie with rocket boosters! Gone were the days of being a ball boy—now he was the one catching the passes, making the moves, and hearing the crowd go wild every time he touched the ball. His first season was solid, but everyone could tell he was just warming up. Larry's career wasn't about being good—it was about being legendary!

In his rookie year, Larry caught 59 passes for 780 yards and eight touchdowns. Not too shabby! But he knew he had more to give. By his second season in 2005, he was tearing through defenses like a hot knife through buttered popcorn. He caught a whopping 103 passes for 1,409 yards and ten touchdowns, earning his first Pro Bowl selection. Fans started calling him "Sticky Fingers" – a perfect nickname for someone who never let go of the ball once it landed in his hands!

Larry's connection with the Cardinals grew stronger each season, just like a superhero's bond with his sidekick. He was known not just for his amazing catches but for his work ethic and humble attitude. He was the guy who stayed late after practice, catching extra passes and working on his skills. He didn't need to—everyone knew he was a star—but for Larry, being great wasn't about what others said. It was about knowing he'd earned it.

Then came the 2008 season, and Larry went into full superhero mode! The Cardinals finished the regular season with a so-so 9-7 record, just sneaking into the playoffs. But once they were in, Larry turned on the turbo jets. In the Wild Card Round, he burned the Atlanta Falcons with six catches for 101 yards and a touchdown. Not bad, right? But he was just getting started. The next week, he absolutely roasted the Carolina Panthers with eight catches for 166 yards, helping the Cardinals win 33–13. Fans were starting to wonder if he was even human!

Then came the NFC Championship game against the Philadelphia Eagles. Larry decided to put on a show for the ages. In the first half alone, he caught three touchdown passes, tying an NFL record for the most touchdown receptions in a playoff game. The crowd went bananas! The Cardinals won 32–25, and suddenly, they were heading to the Super Bowl for the first time ever. Talk about a fairy-tale season!

Super Bowl XLIII was Larry's moment to shine. Playing against the Pittsburgh Steelers, he caught two touchdowns, including an epic 64-yard sprint that put the Cardinals ahead late in the game. For a moment, it looked like Larry had pulled off the ultimate comeback. But the Steelers managed a last-second win, leaving Larry and his teammates with heavy hearts. "Losing was a bitter pill to swallow," he said. But even in defeat, his performance was legendary. He set postseason records for receiving yards, receptions, and touchdowns, surpassing the great Jerry Rice!

Larry's Super Bowl performance wasn't just about numbers. It showed that he could rise to the occasion when it mattered most. His teammates and fans admired him even more because he played with every ounce of heart he had. The next season, he kept the fire burning, catching 97 passes for 1,092 yards and leading the league with 13 touchdowns. People started talking about him as a future Hall of Famer, even though he was only in his sixth season!

Over the years, Larry became a legend on the field, known for jaw-dropping catches that defied logic—the kind that left fans shaking their heads in awe, wondering if he had glue on his gloves or springs in his shoes! It wasn't just his insane talent that made Larry unforgettable. He stood out in a different way: in a world where some NFL stars acted like they owned the universe, Larry was a breath of fresh air. He was known for his kindness, his respect, and his humble spirit. He was the kind of guy who always had time for others, no matter how high he climbed. Dennis Ryan, the Vikings' equipment manager, remembered Larry from way back when he was just a ball boy. "If he wants to borrow some footballs... we're going to get a thank you," Ryan said with a smile. "He's always been that way, and I think he's really a great reflection of his parents."

In 2011, Larry's hard work paid off big time when he signed an enormous eight-year, $120 million contract extension with the Cardinals, putting him among the NFL's highest-paid players. But did the cash change him? Not one bit. Larry stayed laser-focused, putting up big numbers and leading his team through every high and low. His loyalty to the Cardinals was rock-solid. Even when the going got tough, he stuck with them, steady as ever. "I take what I do seriously, and I do not live through my son's success," his dad, Larry Sr., shared. He didn't need to—Larry's achievements spoke volumes all on their own.

As the years rolled on, Larry just kept setting records, one after another. By 2015, he reached an incredible milestone, becoming the youngest player to snag 1,000 career receptions—a feat only the NFL's best could claim. And that season, he reminded everyone of his clutch power in the playoffs. In an unforgettable face-off against the Green Bay Packers, he caught eight passes for a jaw-dropping 176 yards, including a heart-stopping, 75-yard run in overtime that had fans leaping from their seats! Moments later, he capped the drive with a five-yard touchdown catch, sending the Cardinals straight to the NFC Championship game. Once again, Larry had proven he was unstoppable when the game was on the line.

For Larry, the game was never the whole story; there was always something deeper driving him. Football may have been his passion, but his heart had room for so much more. Throughout his career, he dedicated himself to helping others, reaching out beyond the field to make a difference. He founded the Larry Fitzgerald First Down Fund to support kids and families, funding youth camps, donating equipment to schools, and lifting up families in need. In his hometown of Minneapolis, he refurbished local basketball courts and provided new helmets for youth football programs, making sure kids had the resources they needed to dream big.

Larry's giving spirit also honored his mom's legacy. He created the Carol Fitzgerald Memorial Fund in her memory, supporting causes close to her heart, like teaching people about staying healthy and helping those in need. For Larry, giving back wasn't just a nice gesture—it was woven into who he was, a commitment as strong as his drive on the field.

By his 15th season, Larry was no longer the bright-eyed rookie he once was. He had grown into a seasoned veteran, a mentor, and a living legend, respected by teammates and rivals alike. Age didn't slow him down—it just added to his depth, making him an even greater force on and off the field.

When Larry finally hung up his cleats, he left behind a legacy that went far beyond stats and trophies. Yes, the numbers were mind-blowing—over 17,000 receiving yards, 121 touchdowns, 11 Pro Bowl selections. He'd been named to the NFL's All-Decade Team for the 2010s and was hailed as one of the greatest wide receivers to ever play. But to Larry, the stats were only a chapter in his story. What mattered most was the life he led, one filled with kindness, humility, and a big heart. In his own words, "Catching touchdowns, running companies, recording songs ... might be a sign that you're great at doing something, but greatness is not just about doing. It's about being." He proved his greatness by being a role model, a leader, and an all-around good guy.

Jerry Rice

THE RELENTLESS PURSUIT OF GREATNESS

The story of Jerry Rice begins in a tiny, blink-and-you-miss-it town called Crawford, MS, where the air smelled like fresh hay, the sun beat down like it was mad at the earth, and you could hear the crunch of gravel roads for miles. This place had about as many people as your average school cafeteria during lunchtime, and everyone knew everyone. The local gossip? Probably about which cow wandered off whose farm this time.

Jerry was born way back in 1962—yeah, that's so long ago, phones definitely still had tails attached to walls. The sixth of eight kids in a family so big, they probably needed a group huddle just to decide what was for dinner. His dad, Joe, was a brick mason—a man who didn't just lay bricks but seemed to be made of them. Jerry said, "My dad was a tough man." Tough like "don't-you-dare-complain-about-hauling-these-bricks" tough. Joe worked long hours building houses, and when there was more work than he could handle, guess who got dragged in as the backup crew? That's right: Jerry and his brothers.

Every morning in the sticky Mississippi heat, young Jerry stood on top of scaffolds, catching bricks like his life depended on it. He had hands as quick as a lightning bolt and the focus of a hawk stalking dinner. This wasn't playtime; this was "don't-drop-it-or-you'll-hear-about-it-all-week" time. And that bricklaying wasn't just about bricks—it was about shaping Jerry's work ethic. "It taught me the meaning of hard work." He says. But let's be honest, it probably also taught him that bricks are heavy, and if he didn't find a different career, he'd spend his whole life covered in mortar dust.

When Jerry wasn't dodging a scolding from his dad for slacking on the job, he was getting into his own brand of mischief. You know that kid who always seems to be two steps away from trouble? That was Jerry. He liked to run—literally. Running wasn't some hobby; it was a survival tactic. One time in high school, Jerry decided school was too boring for his taste and tried to ditch class. Big mistake. His assistant principal spotted him sneaking out and shouted, "Hey, you, stop right there!" Now, most kids might've given up at that point, but not Jerry. He took off like a cheetah chasing its dinner.

The principal couldn't believe what he was seeing. Jerry's legs pumped so fast, they practically kicked up dust clouds. After the principal finally caught him, he didn't yell. He made a surprising offer: *"You're fast, boy. You're going to join the football team."* Jerry groaned. Football? Was this supposed to be a punishment? At the time, Jerry had no plans to become a football player. Honestly, he probably thought, *Great, now I have to run for fun and get yelled at by a coach instead of my dad*. But that principal saw something special in Jerry—something Jerry himself didn't see yet.

At first, football practice was just another chore for Jerry, like hauling bricks or picking cotton on the farm (which, by the way, he also had to do). But soon enough, he started loving the game. He got to run, he got to catch, and he didn't have to haul anything heavier than a football. And unlike bricks, footballs don't hurt when they smack you in the face.

Okay, sometimes they do, but Jerry was fast enough to avoid that. Plus, it was way more fun juking defenders than it was dodging his dad's critiques about sloppy mortar.

Jerry's mom, Eddie, wasn't as thrilled about his football adventures at first. She thought the sport was too rough, and honestly, she wasn't wrong. But Jerry's determination couldn't be stopped. He said, "The more my mom fought it, the more determined I was, so she gave it up." That was Eddie's way of saying, *Fine, but don't come crying to me when you get tackled.* Heads up: Jerry didn't cry. He thrived.

Jerry played multiple positions for his high school football team: running back, tight end, defensive back, you name it. But it was as a wide receiver where he truly shined. His hands, already trained by years of catching bricks, were magnetic. It was like the football would see Jerry coming and think, *Well, I guess I live here now.* People started calling him a natural. But Jerry? He knew better. It wasn't natural talent; it was sweat, grit, and all those afternoons spent outrunning trouble.

When he wasn't on the field, Jerry found time to bond with his siblings. They made a pact—Jerry and his older brother—that one of them would make it big and buy their parents a house. They didn't know how they'd pull it off, but it became their family's unspoken dream. Years later, Jerry said, "One of the greatest thrills of my life was bringing my parents to the Super Bowl and having them experience it." But back then, they weren't dreaming about Super Bowls. They were dreaming about getting through another Mississippi summer without melting.

During his junior and senior years, Jerry leveled up. He started running home after practice—five miles in the Mississippi humidity—because he didn't have a ride. Who needs a ride when you've got legs that could outrun half the town? His dedication showed on the field. By his senior year, Jerry had become a Mississippi All-State wide receiver. His catches were so smooth, so precise, his high school coach once said, "You throw the ball anywhere near Jerry, and he'll catch it." It was like Jerry had a secret deal with gravity.

But even with all his talent, Jerry didn't get much attention from big-time colleges. Schools like Mississippi State and Ole Miss overlooked him. Maybe they thought a kid from Crawford couldn't make it big. That changed when a coach named Archie Cooley from Mississippi Valley State University showed up. Cooley was known for running a pass-heavy offense—so pass-heavy, in fact, people called him "The Gunslinger." When he saw Jerry play, Cooley didn't hesitate. "That kid has magic hands," he said. Cooley offered Jerry a spot on the team, and just like that, Jerry was off to college in Itta Bena, Mississippi.

And so, young Jerry left behind the dusty roads of Crawford, the bricklaying, and even his mom's stern warnings about football being "too rough." But he carried with him everything he'd learned in that small town: the work ethic, the hunger to prove himself, and the determination to do something big for his family. It wasn't the end of his story—not even close. But it was the beginning of something legendary.

When Jerry showed up at Mississippi Valley University, It was a small school that hardly made a splash in the football world. It wasn't even a middleweight. In fact, you probably wouldn't have known the school *had* a football team unless you tripped over their equipment on campus. The Delta Devils played on a field that was as humble as the school itself—some days, it probably doubled as a cow pasture. But none of that mattered to Jerry. He wasn't looking for bright lights or big-name schools. He was looking for a chance to prove himself. And under the guidance of Coach Archie Cooley, he got exactly that.

Now, Cooley wasn't your average coach. This guy ran an offense so wild it might as well have been designed by a kid who spent too much time playing Madden. People called it the "Satellite Express." Why? Because it involved throwing the ball *constantly*. Picture a football flying through the air on every single play. That was Cooley's game plan. And guess who became the star of this aerial circus? Jerry Rice. "They assured me the ball was going to be in the air," Jerry said, "and it was up to me to prove to everyone I could be a professional athlete."

The partnership between Jerry and freshman quarterback Willie Totten was a match made in football heaven. Together, they became known as "The Satellite Express," the most dangerous duo to ever light up a scoreboard in the Southwestern Athletic Conference. Totten threw, and Jerry caught. Again, and again, and again. Defensive backs? They couldn't touch Jerry. It was like trying to catch smoke with a butterfly net. By his sophomore season, Jerry had already racked up 66 catches for 1,133 yards and seven touchdowns. Not bad for a kid who wasn't even sure he wanted to play football.

But let's talk about 1983. That was the year Jerry Rice turned into a human highlight reel. He didn't just break records—he smashed them into tiny little pieces. That season, he caught 102 passes for 1,450 yards and 22 touchdowns. To put that in perspective, most wide receivers would've framed those stats and retired right there. Jerry? He was just warming up. In one game, he caught 24 passes against Southern University. That's right—*24*! At some point, the defense probably just thought, "Eh, let's grab some popcorn and watch this guy go." His hands were so reliable that teammates nicknamed him "World," because it seemed like he could catch anything in the world.

By 1984, his senior season, Jerry had fully transformed into a football legend-in-the-making. He broke his own NCAA records with 112 catches for 1,845 yards and an almost comical 28 touchdowns. Yep, you heard that right. Twenty-eight touchdowns in eleven games. That's more than some NFL teams score in a season. Mississippi Valley State were blowing teams off the field. The Delta Devils averaged over 60 points a game, which is less like football and more like basketball. Even Jerry's coach, Archie Cooley, couldn't hide his awe. "We'd just get the ball to Jerry and watch the magic happen," he said.

But Jerry wasn't only a numbers guy—he thrived under pressure. In the Blue–Gray Classic, an all-star game played on Christmas Day, he faced off against players from powerhouse schools. This was his chance to show the world that a kid from a tiny school in Mississippi could hang with the big boys. Guess what? He didn't just keep up—he took over like a boss. He caught four passes for 101 yards, including a dazzling 60-yard touchdown, and earned MVP honors. The scouts were officially paying attention now.

Still, there were doubters. Some NFL teams looked at Jerry's 40-yard dash time and said he wasn't fast enough. One scout even muttered, "He'll never survive against NFL defenses." Clearly, this guy had never seen Jerry outrun a principal or dodge bricks. But there was one man who believed in Jerry from the start: Bill Walsh, head coach of the San Francisco 49ers. Walsh had been flipping through TV channels one night when he stumbled upon highlights of Jerry torching defenders like a fire-breathing dragon. His first thought? *We need that guy.*

The 1985 NFL Draft rolled around, and Jerry was watching from his brother's tiny apartment in Jackson, Mississippi. He didn't host a big party—he wasn't the kind of guy to count his chickens before they hatched. He hoped the Dallas Cowboys, his childhood favorite team, might draft him with the 17th pick. But then, something unexpected happened. The 49ers traded up to the 16th pick and snagged Jerry right before the Cowboys could. Jerry was stunned. He later admitted, "I started thinking about all the great players on the 49ers—Joe Montana, Ronnie Lott, Dwight Clark. I wondered, 'Where am I going to fit in with this team?'" It didn't take long for Jerry to find out.

When he arrived in San Francisco, the adjustment wasn't easy. Jerry was a small-town kid in a big city, surrounded by bright lights and high expectations. In his first preseason games, he dropped so many passes that fans started calling him a bust. Ouch. The media piled on, too, asking questions like, "Why did Bill Walsh draft this kid from a no-name school?" Jerry admitted, "I wanted to prove myself so much that I overdid it." But here's the thing about Jerry Rice: he never let failure define him. He leaned on his teammates—legends like Joe Montana and Dwight Clark—who told him, "You're going to be the greatest receiver who ever played the game. Just keep working."

And work he did. Jerry became the first guy on the practice field and the last one to leave. He studied film like it was the final exam for a class called "How to Torch Defenders 101." Slowly but surely, the drops disappeared. By the time the regular season rolled around, Jerry was starting to flash the brilliance that had made him a college legend. In one game against the Rams, he exploded for 241 yards—setting a 49ers single-game record. That year, he finished his rookie season with 927 receiving yards, a team record for a rookie. Jerry was a tornado with no off switch. The pressure of being "the kid from the small school" didn't break him. If anything, it made him sharper. He once said, "I didn't want to let my family down. I didn't want to let my teammates down. I just kept pushing."

By the end of his rookie season, everyone knew this kid was special. The doubters? They were eating their words. The fans? They were chanting his name. And Bill Walsh? He looked like a genius. Jerry Rice wasn't a question mark anymore. He was the exclamation point that the 49ers needed. As Jerry entered his second season, the world of professional football had no idea what was coming. But one thing was certain: the Satellite Express had officially left the station, and Jerry Rice was about to take his game to the stratosphere.

By the time Jerry Rice stepped into his second NFL season in 1986, he had moved beyond running routes—he was running *the show*. The rookie jitters? Gone. The dropped passes?

History. All that was left was Jerry Rice, the football-catching machine who could make defenders look like they were stuck in quicksand. And believe me, *nobody* wanted to get stuck in a Jerry Rice highlight reel. That season, Jerry set the NFL ablaze with a jaw-dropping 1,570 receiving yards. If you're wondering how much that is, let me put it this way: it's enough yards to make defensive coordinators lose sleep for months. Jerry didn't just *join* the NFL—he took it over.

Now, let's talk about 1987. This was the year Jerry Rice decided to break the league, one touchdown at a time. It was a strike-shortened season, with only 12 games, but Jerry didn't need a full season to rewrite the record books. He snagged 22 receiving touchdowns, setting an NFL record that still makes jaws drop to this day. "It wasn't about me," Jerry said, "it was about helping my team win." Sure, Jerry, but let's be real—you made winning look *way* too easy. Defenders chasing Jerry were like kids chasing an ice cream truck—always a step too slow.

The next few years were a golden era for Jerry and the San Francisco 49ers. With Joe Montana throwing spirals so perfect they should've been framed in an art museum, Jerry was unstoppable. Together, they became the dynamic duo of the NFL. Montana would throw, Jerry would catch, and the crowd would roar so loud you'd think the stadium might collapse.

At 26 years old, Jerry caught the longest pass of his career—a 96-yard bomb from Montana that left defenders tripping over their own feet. It was like watching a rocket launch, except the rocket was wearing a #80 jersey. That same season, Jerry and the 49ers capped it all off with a nail-biting Super Bowl win over the Cincinnati Bengals. And guess who walked away with the Super Bowl MVP trophy? Yep, Jerry. He caught 11 passes for 215 yards, a performance so dominant that even the Bengals' coach probably clapped out of sheer respect.

The next year, the 49ers returned to the Super Bowl, this time obliterating the Denver Broncos 55–10. That game wasn't just a victory—it was a massacre. Jerry caught seven passes for 148 yards and three touchdowns, cementing his reputation as the guy who showed up when the lights were brightest. Super Bowl records? Jerry collected them like kids collect Pokémon cards.

By the early 1990s, Jerry Rice transformed—now he was THE football player. Joe Montana had handed the quarterback reins to Steve Young, and the Rice-Young combo proved just as lethal. In 1994, Jerry hit a milestone that left fans in awe: he broke Jim Brown's record for career touchdowns, scoring his 127th touchdown in a game against the Los Angeles Raiders. When Jerry stepped into the end zone, you could almost hear the record books groan, "Not again!"

And then came Super Bowl XXIX in 1995. Jerry wasn't feeling great the night before the game, but you'd never know it from his performance. He caught ten passes for 149 yards and three touchdowns, helping the 49ers demolish the San Diego Chargers 49–26. Oh, and by the way, that marked Jerry's *third* Super Bowl ring. If you're counting, that's one for each hand, plus a spare. That year, he delivered one of the greatest seasons ever by a wide receiver. He hauled in 122 catches for a staggering 1,848 yards and 15 touchdowns, setting an NFL record for most receiving yards in a single season. That record stood for nearly two decades. He even had a game against the Minnesota Vikings where he torched them for 289 yards. That's not a football game—that's a one-man fireworks show.

Through all the accolades and records, Jerry's work ethic remained legendary. He ran *perfect* routes. He trained like his life depended on it. And then there was "The Hill," a 2.5-mile monster in Edgewood County Park that Jerry sprinted up during the offseason. Teammates who tried running it with him usually regretted their life choices about halfway up. Ricky Watters, a Pro Bowl running back, once joined Jerry for a run. When Jerry sprinted the last 800 meters, Ricky was so far behind, he might as well have been in a different zip code. "That's when I knew Jerry was on another level," Watters admitted.

Even injuries couldn't slow him down. In 1997, he tore two ligaments in his left knee during the season opener—a devastating injury for most players. But Jerry wasn't like most players. Just 14 weeks later, he returned to the field and scored a touchdown. Let me repeat that: he came back in 14 weeks from an injury that should've sidelined him for a year. "It's not about how hard you get hit," Jerry said. "It's about how hard you work to get back up."

By 2000, after 16 astonishing seasons with the San Francisco 49ers—seasons filled with unforgettable Super Bowls, impossible catches, and a catalog of records so long it could double as a library index—Jerry Rice faced what many believed would be the twilight of his career. But Jerry wasn't interested in twilight. Twilight fades. Twilight goes quietly.

Jerry Rice didn't *do* quiet. So, when he signed with the Oakland Raiders, people braced themselves, curious if the old legend had any fire left. Turns out, Jerry had a raging inferno.

Let's paint this picture clearly: most NFL players in their late 30s are already home on Sundays, watching games from a recliner, knees wrapped in ice packs. Jerry? Even at 39, he wasn't slowing down; he was speeding up. He caught 92 passes for 1,211 yards and scored seven touchdowns that season—numbers that would've been impressive for a player in their prime, let alone someone old enough to be referred to as "the veteran" with reverence by rookies who grew up watching him. Forty years old? still unstoppable! And when he helped the Raiders reach the Super Bowl that season, it wasn't a comeback story. It was a *refusal* to ever leave the conversation. Jerry Rice didn't believe in stepping aside; he believed in stepping up.

Think about it. Forty years old. Catching passes from a new quarterback, running routes sharper than kids half his age, and doing it all with that same burning hunger he had as a teenager hauling bricks in Crawford. Watching him play was like watching a superhero movie, except this wasn't Hollywood. It was real. Jerry didn't wear a cape—he wore #80. And while defenders desperately tried to keep up, fans couldn't help but wonder, "How is he still this good?" It wasn't magic. It wasn't luck. It was work. The kind of work most people wouldn't dream of doing, even for a week, let alone for 20 years.

But Jerry's time in the NFL wasn't just about the *what*—the touchdowns, the catches, the championships—it was about the *how*. How he played every game as if the world was watching. How he trained in the offseason like he was still a rookie trying to make the team. How he treated the game with reverence, like it wasn't just a sport but a sacred trust. "It's not about being the best," Jerry said. "It's about giving your best every single day." And that's what made him extraordinary. Jerry didn't just *show* you what greatness looked like—he *dragged* you into believing you could find it in yourself, too.

When Jerry finally stepped off the field for the last time, the NFL lost a force of nature. His career numbers—1,549 catches, 22,895 receiving yards, 197 receiving touchdowns—they were monument records. They weren't built overnight. They were built brick by brick, yard by yard, catch by catch, with a ferocity that never waned. They were so massive, so untouchable, they felt less like statistics and more like something etched onto the side of a mountain. And yet, for all the glory of the numbers, what made Jerry truly unforgettable wasn't the stats. It was the story. The story of a kid from Crawford, Mississippi, who grew up catching bricks with hands so steady they'd one day be compared to magnets. It was the story of a player who didn't let early struggles define him but instead let them fuel him. It was the story of a man who ran every route in practice like the Super Bowl depended on it and inspired everyone around him to raise their game just by being there. From Joe Montana to Steve Young, from Bill Walsh to Rich Gannon, his teammates and coaches did respect him but also followed his lead.

And then there were the fans. Oh, the fans. They *believed* in him. He gave them hope, week after week, season after season, year after year. Watching Jerry Rice was about witnessing what happens when you refuse to settle for less than your absolute best. It was about seeing someone defy expectations so thoroughly that he didn't just raise the bar—he *became* the bar.

The end came not with a curtain call but with a quiet dignity that matched Jerry's unrelenting focus. Every touchdown, every route, every sprint up "The Hill" was part of the goodbye he'd been writing for 20 years. And when the NFL Hall of Fame came calling—as everyone knew it would—they practically built a new wing in his honor. And for all of us who grew up watching #80 dance down the sideline, make impossible catches, and shatter barriers, one thing is certain: the game will never see another Jerry Rice.

Reggie White

THE MINISTER OF DEFENSE

Reggie White bursts into the world on December 19, 1961, in Chattanooga, Tennessee, with a laugh so loud that the nurses probably assumed he was born telling a joke. His mother, Thelma Collier, held him close and probably wondered if she'd just given birth to a linebacker instead of a baby. Even as a toddler, Reggie was bigger than everyone else around him. By age five, he was towering over the other kids like a sunflower in a patch of daisies, grinning from ear to ear as they tried to climb him like a jungle gym.

By the time Reggie turns 12 in 1973, something extraordinary happens. One day, he looks up from a football in the backyard and tells his mom, "Mama, I'm gonna be two things when I grow up: a football player and a preacher." His mom smiles but probably hides a little laugh because, seriously, how many kids even *think* like that at twelve? Most are too busy asking for extra snacks or trying to convince their parents they need a pet iguana. But Reggie isn't like most kids. He's already thinking big—like, *NFL and Heaven-level big*.

And it wasn't just talk. Sundays were special for the White family. They'd get dressed up for church, and little Reggie, sitting in the pews, listened to the preachers like he was studying game tape. He loved their fiery passion, their booming voices, and how they could get a whole room of people cheering, clapping, and saying, "Amen!" Reggie would sit there wide-eyed, probably thinking, "I can do that, but maybe louder." His faith didn't come from one dramatic moment; it grew quietly, like a strong oak tree. Years later, he would say, "I've always believed since I was a kid that God was gonna allow me to play professional football, to use it as a platform to proclaim and live out the name of Jesus."

Way before the NFL spotlight ever found him, there's Howard High School. Howard High in the 1970s was the *Reggie White Show*. And trust me, you didn't need a ticket to watch. Reggie was *huge*. At 6 feet 5 inches and nearly 300 pounds, he looked like someone had accidentally built a high schooler out of bricks and steel beams. His classmates gave him nicknames like "Bigfoot" and "Land of the Giant," and if you're thinking, "Wow, that sounds kind of mean," don't worry—Reggie laughed harder than anyone. "Kids used to call me Bigfoot," he said once. "They'd tease me and run away. Around seventh grade, I found something I was good at. I could play football."

And *play football* he did. Under Coach Robert Pulliam's guidance, Reggie turned into an unstoppable force on the field. Opposing players must've felt like they were trying to stop a bulldozer with a bicycle. By his senior year, Reggie is racking up stats so ridiculous they sound like something out of a video game: 140 tackles and 10 sacks in one season. Yes, you read that right—*140 tackles*! You know how in cartoons someone always gets flattened by a steamroller? That was Reggie. Except instead of flattening people, he'd tackle them clean, then help them up and probably ask how their mom was doing.

Of course, even as the crowd cheered for his tackles and sacks, that wasn't enough for Reggie. He also had a second job. Every Sunday, he took to local churches in Chattanooga to deliver sermons. Imagine a 17-year-old, fresh off the football field, standing at the pulpit preaching to a room full of adults. He'd deliver fiery, passionate sermons, mixing Bible verses with humor and honesty. One time, while giving a sermon, he said, "God places the heaviest burden on those who can carry its weight." Now, imagine hearing that wisdom come out of a teenager! And people believed him.

But not everyone was thrilled about Reggie's talents. His opponents on the football field had a slightly different opinion. They probably sat in their huddles, groaning, "Why *me*? Why do I have to block *him*?" But you couldn't really blame them. Facing Reggie White was like trying to tackle a bear that could also quote scripture.

Now, Reggie wasn't all football and preaching. He had a softer side too. He loved his mom fiercely and often told her, "One day, I'm gonna take care of you for the rest of your life." And if you knew Reggie, you'd know he meant it. His mom, Thelma, had worked hard to raise him, and Reggie never forgot that. She was his rock, his number-one fan, and his best friend. One time, when Reggie came home from practice covered in mud and sweat, Thelma looked him up and down and said, "Boy, you're too big for me to wash all that." Reggie grinned and replied, "Well, Mama, you said God won't give us more than we can handle, so here I am." Thelma laughed so hard she almost dropped the laundry basket.

As Reggie wrapped up his high school years, recruiters from colleges all over the country were practically camping on his lawn, begging him to join their teams. Everyone wanted him. But Reggie didn't want to stray too far from home, and so he chose the University of Tennessee, keeping his orange-and-white dreams close to his Tennessee roots. And as for Chattanooga? The city couldn't have been prouder of its gentle giant. They cheered him on from the stands and from the pews, knowing he was destined for something extraordinary. They did see a football player; but they also saw a kid with big dreams and an even bigger heart.

Reggie White rolls into the University of Tennessee in 1980 like a freight train carrying both a Bible and a playbook. It's not a quiet arrival. He's got his big frame, an even bigger personality, and a mission: to dominate the football field *and* save some souls while he's at it. You can practically hear his internal monologue as he walks into Neyland Stadium for the first time: "I'm here to hit quarterbacks and preach scripture—and I'm all out of scripture for today." Okay, maybe not, but you get the idea. Reggie isn't wasting any time.

As a freshman, Reggie wastes no time earning his spot on the team. By the end of the season, he's not only a starter on the defensive line but also a wrecking ball of a player. He records 51 tackles, two sacks, and even blocks a punt, which helps Tennessee score its first touchdown in a win against Georgia Tech. That's right—*block a punt*. Let's be honest, if Reggie White came charging at you, you wouldn't just miss your kick; you'd probably rethink your life choices. The coaches are so impressed that they give him the Andy Spiva Award for the "Most Improved Defensive Player." Reggie, ever humble, probably shrugs and says, "Well, I just did what God blessed me to do."

By his sophomore year in 1981, Reggie is a one-man demolition crew. Quarterbacks are waking up in cold sweats, dreaming of Reggie sprinting toward them. He racks up a team-leading 8 sacks, 95 tackles, and somehow still finds time to block *three* extra points. At this point, the opposing teams probably want to petition the NCAA to start playing with *two* footballs: one for the game and one to throw as a distraction for Reggie. But no decoy works on him. When Tennessee takes on Memphis State, Reggie has 10 tackles and two sacks, one of which results in a safety. The announcers start calling him "outstanding," and the fans call him a hero. But Reggie? He says, "God places the heaviest burden on those who can carry its weight."

Oh, and did I mention he's still preaching on Sundays? While most college kids are hitting the snooze button after Saturday-night pizza binges, Reggie is standing at a pulpit in a suit, telling a congregation that their faith needs to be as strong as their defense on third down. "One thing that God revealed to me," Reggie tells them, "is that we as Christians are going to have to get a portion of the media so we can present the good news." You'd think people would chuckle at a 19-year-old saying this, but with Reggie's booming voice and conviction, they listen.

With such an extraordinary sophomore season, the expectations for Reggie are sky-high heading into his junior year in 1982. But in fact, it was actually rough. He suffers an ankle injury, and for most players, that might mean taking it easy for a season. But Reggie? He plays through it anyway, leading the team with 7 sacks and still managing 47 tackles—because apparently, Reggie's idea of "injured" still involves making other teams cry. His standout moment comes in a tie game against LSU, where he racks up 8 tackles, a sack, and a crucial fourth-down stop. Oh, and he also scares Iowa in the Peach Bowl with 8 tackles, 2 sacks, and a forced fumble. You'd think the quarterbacks might start wearing "Do Not Disturb" signs when Reggie's on the field, but there's no escape from him.

By now, Tennessee fans have nicknamed him the "Minister of Defense," and it's sticking like super glue. The name is perfect because, on the field, Reggie *defends* like his life depends on it, and off the field, he's literally preaching the Word of God. One time, a local reporter asks him about his football style. Reggie grins and says, "Sacks are great, but I'm not here to chase stats. I want to hit the quarterback clean, play fair, and glorify God in everything I do."

And then comes 1983—Reggie's senior year. A storm nobody saw coming. He dominates like never before. This is the year where Reggie seems to say, "You know what? I think I'll break every record in the book." He ends the season with a jaw-dropping 15 sacks, setting a single-season school record that would last *33 years*. Thirty-three years—that's an era, not a stat! And that's just the sacks. He also tallies 100 tackles, 9 tackles for loss, and an interception, because why not? He's Reggie White. He can do everything except *stop being awesome*. Plus, there's one game in particular that makes everyone sit up and take notice. Tennessee's clash with LSU. It is so wild that the SEC has to sit up and take notice. Reggie records 12 tackles and 3 sacks in a single game, earning him the "Southeast Lineman of the Week" award. But the best part? Tennessee beats Alabama 41–34, and Reggie sacks their quarterback Walter Lewis twice. At this point, you have to imagine quarterbacks are avoiding eye contact with Reggie in the post-game handshake line. If they could, they'd probably send their apologies in a thank-you card instead.

When Tennessee plays Maryland in the Florida Citrus Bowl, Reggie delivers one of the most iconic moments of his college career. Maryland's quarterback Boomer Esiason (yes, the future NFL star) gets sacked by Reggie so hard that he probably sees the future—and it looks like Reggie's face. Tennessee wins 30–23, and fans celebrate like they've just won the Super Bowl.

By the end of the season, Reggie is a *consensus All-American* and is named SEC Player of the Year. He finishes his college career with 293 tackles, 32 sacks, and countless broken dreams for opposing offensive lines. His records stand for decades. To this day, Tennessee fans say his name with a kind of reverence usually reserved for legends and superheroes.

During his years at Tennessee, our champ is as much a leader off the field as he is on it. His teammates look up to him, not just because he can bench-press an entire offensive line, but because he's a genuinely good guy. He's the kind of player who'd flatten someone during a game, then help them up and probably offer them a ride home. One of his coaches says later, "He was the heart of our team—on the field, in the locker room, and in life."

It's 1984, and Reggie White is leaving Tennessee, but don't for one second think this is a sad goodbye. No, sir. Reggie doesn't leave anywhere quietly. With 293 tackles and 32 sacks in his college career, he's basically got NFL teams lining up at his doorstep. But hold your horses, NFL—Reggie isn't coming to you just yet. Instead, he surprises everyone and signs a *five-year, $4 million contract* with the Memphis Showboats of the upstart United States Football League (USFL). Why? Because Reggie loves Tennessee, and the Showboats give him the chance to stay close to home. Plus, let's be honest: who wouldn't want to play for a team named after riverboats? It sounds like the perfect mix of football and fun.

So, there he is in Memphis, playing for a team that feels like it was pulled straight out of a cowboy movie. And Reggie doesn't disappoint. Over two seasons with the Showboats, he starts every game and racks up 23.5 sacks. let that number do the talking—23.5 sacks in *two* seasons! That's like trying to count popcorn kernels in a microwave. Reggie also records a safety and forces a fumble that gets returned for a touchdown. By now, the offensive linemen in the USFL probably start each game praying, "Dear God, let me survive Reggie White." And if anyone on the field tries to trash-talk him, Reggie's response is pure poetry. He doesn't trash-talk back—he just smiles and hits harder. If you were lucky, you'd also get a Bible verse after he flattened you. Talk about multitasking.

But even while he's tearing it up on the field, the USFL is struggling. The league isn't exactly what you'd call "financially stable." Some teams can barely pay their players. Meanwhile, Reggie, ever the planner, keeps an eye on the horizon. He knows the NFL is watching him like a hawk, and soon enough, opportunity comes knocking.

In 1985, the USFL folds like a bad poker hand, and Reggie lands with the Philadelphia Eagles after being selected in the NFL's supplemental draft. But here's the catch: The Eagles are broke-ish. To sign Reggie, they have to *buy out* the remaining years of his

Memphis contract. The total deal? Four years for $1.85 million. That's less money than he made in Memphis, but Reggie doesn't care. Why? Because he's about to play in the *NFL*, baby! And he's ready to show the league what "The Minister of Defense" is all about.

Reggie arrives in Philadelphia halfway through the 1985 season, and from the moment he steps onto the field, he's a human wrecking ball in green and white. In his very first game, he records 10 tackles and 2.5 sacks. Yep, in just one game. By the end of the season, he's racked up 13 sacks in 13 games, earning him the title of NFC Defensive Rookie of the Year. That's right: the rookie who was "unproven" now has quarterbacks across the league considering early retirement.

The thing about Reggie is that it feels like he bends the rules of football into something only he can play. By 1986, under the infamous head coach Buddy Ryan, Reggie becomes the centerpiece of the Eagles' defense, which, let's be honest, is more like a wrecking crew. Ryan calls him "the best defensive lineman I've ever been around," and coming from the guy who coached the 1985 Chicago Bears, that's saying something. Reggie racks up 18 sacks in 1986, dominating games with his signature mix of speed, strength, and a football IQ so sharp you'd think he studied game tapes in his sleep.

But the 1987 season is where Reggie does something no one has ever seen before—or since. The NFL players go on strike, which shortens the season to just 12 games, but that doesn't slow Reggie down. Instead, he sets an *Eagles franchise record* with 21 sacks. Let me repeat that: 21 sacks in *12 games*. That's an average of 1.75 sacks per game, a record that still stands. Quarterbacks are so terrified that they probably start asking their offensive linemen, "Hey, is it legal to bring pepper spray onto the field?"

When Reggie sacks quarterbacks, he does it with a flair that sets the tone for everything that follows. One of his most famous moves is the "hump move." Imagine this: Reggie charges at a lineman, then uses his freakish strength to lift the guy off his feet and toss him aside like an empty soda can. If you ever wonder what it feels like to be "humped" by Reggie White, the answer is: humiliating. And probably painful. But here's the thing about Reggie that makes him more than just a football player: he's a leader, both on and off the field. In Philadelphia, he's a star athlete and a living example of what it means to be a role model. He spends his free time preaching on street corners in the city's toughest neighborhoods. He donates money to Christian outreach programs and spends hours talking to kids about faith, hard work, and staying out of trouble. "I believe that I've been blessed with physical ability in order to gain a platform to preach the gospel," Reggie says. And he means it. He preaches to his teammates, to the fans, and to anyone who will listen—because for Reggie, football is a platform, not a destination.

Oh, and don't think he takes himself too seriously. Reggie is famous for his sense of humor. One of his teammates once recalled how Reggie would yell Bible verses at opposing linemen right before the snap. "The Lord is my shepherd!" he'd shout. Then he'd plow through them like a bulldozer. One time, offensive tackle Harris Barton tried to throw Reggie off his game by saying, "Reggie, I'm Jewish!" Reggie burst into laughter right there on the field. He was a ferocious competitor, sure, but he also had this huge, joyful personality that made everyone love him—even the guys he bulldozed.

Over the next eight seasons with the Eagles, Reggie cements his legacy as one of the greatest defensive players in NFL history. By the time he leaves the team in 1992, he's recorded 124 sacks, making him the Eagles' all-time sack leader—a record that stands for almost three decades. But Reggie's impact isn't just in the stats. It's in the way he inspires his teammates, fans, and city. He's more than a player; he's a symbol of hope.

Then, in 1993, Reggie becomes a *free agent*. Back then, free agency is still brand-new—so new, in fact, that nobody is entirely sure how it works yet. And suddenly, the NFL becomes one giant race to sign the "Minister of Defense." Everyone wants him. It's about changing a team's future. Reggie has spent years dominating on the field and uplifting communities off it, and now every franchise sees him as the ultimate cornerstone.

The recruitment process? Absolute chaos. Teams practically throw themselves at Reggie. The Browns send a private jet, the Falcons promise to build him a church, and the 49ers offer him dinners at elite restaurants. Packers head coach Mike Holmgren leaves a voicemail for Reggie that's so bold, it becomes legendary: "Reggie, this is God. Go to Green Bay." And to the surprise of everyone, It works, Reggie *does* go to Green Bay—a tiny city with a population smaller than some stadiums, where the winters are brutal, and the team hasn't seen glory since the Lombardi days. The deal—four years, $17 million—is one of the richest in NFL history for a defensive player at the time. But it's about more than money. Reggie sees something special in Green Bay: a chance to be part of a team that can win it all. And let's not forget his faith. Reggie later says he prayed for guidance, and he truly believed Green Bay was where God wanted him to go.

When Reggie arrives in Green Bay, the Packers are... well, not great. The team hasn't won a championship since the days of Vince Lombardi, and Green Bay itself, with its tiny population and freezing winters, is considered a tough sell for top players—especially African American players. In 1993, the city has fewer than 500 Black residents. But Reggie changes everything. He did transform the entire *culture*.

From the moment he puts on that green and gold jersey, Reggie elevates the Packers to another level. In his first season, he records 13 sacks and leads a defense that goes from one of the league's worst to one of its best. Teammates describe him as a "gentle giant," a man who could destroy a quarterback on Sunday and then lead a Bible study on Monday. Wide receiver Andre Rison later says, "Reggie showed us all what it meant to live with purpose." But it's in 1996 that everything comes together. That year, the Packers become a powerhouse, led by Reggie, head coach Mike Holmgren, and a gunslinging quarterback named Brett Favre. The defense is the best in the league, and Reggie is its beating heart. In Super Bowl XXXI, the Packers face off against the New England Patriots, and Reggie owns the field. He sets a Super Bowl record with three sacks, practically living in the Patriots' backfield. The Packers win 35–21, and for Reggie, it's the culmination of everything he's worked for. It's his first championship at any level, and when the confetti rains down, you can see the joy on his face. He later says, "Whatsoever thy hand findeth to do, do it with thy might," quoting a verse that guided him throughout his career.

Reggie plays two more seasons with the Packers, and in 1998, he's named NFL Defensive Player of the Year for the second time—at the age of 37! Even as he nears the end of his career, Reggie is still unstoppable. When he retires (for the first time) in 1999, he leaves behind a Green Bay team that has gone from underdog to perennial contender, and fans who look up to him like a true hero.

In 2000, just when it seemed Reggie's story had reached its final chapter, he stuns everyone by suiting up for one last season with the Carolina Panthers. Retirement? Wait a second. At 39 years old, when most players are content with broadcasting gigs, Reggie straps on the pads one more time. People wonder if he can still hang with players nearly half his age. Reggie's answer? Absolutely. He walks into Carolina's locker room like a veteran gladiator, calm and unshaken, ready to show that greatness doesn't fade. That season, Reggie starts all 16 games, let alone someone pushing 40 and facing the brutal trenches of the NFL. He's still a wrecking ball too. He records 5.5 sacks, disrupts offensive lines like clockwork, and commands double-teams like he's 25 all over again. Teammates are in awe of his relentless work ethic and how he mentors younger players, many of whom grew up idolizing him. Opposing quarterbacks? Well, they quickly learn that even a 39-year-old Reggie White can make their Sundays miserable. When the season ends, Reggie decides it's finally time to hang up his cleats for good, leaving the NFL with 198 career sacks, the second-most in league history at the time. Counting his USFL years, his total rises to 221.5 sacks, making him the all-time professional football sacks leader.

Off the field, Reggie continues to inspire. He spends his post-football years traveling the country, preaching and spreading his faith. In 1996, after arsonists burn down the Inner City Church in Knoxville, Tennessee, where Reggie served as an associate minister, he helps raise money to rebuild it. He also stars in the Christian movie *Reggie's Prayer*, playing—you guessed it—a retired football player who becomes a high school coach. (Bonus: Brett Favre makes a cameo as a janitor!)

Reggie also spends his time helping others, rebuilding African American churches that were targeted in hate crimes and supporting communities in need. He and his wife, Sara, build shelters for unwed mothers and fund community development projects in Tennessee. Reggie does both preach and live his faith. As he once said, "The Bible says, 'Faith without works is dead.' That is just another way of saying, 'Put your money where your mouth is.'"

In 2006, Reggie White steps into the Pro Football Hall of Fame, where greatness like his belongs. His number 92 is celebrated by both the Eagles and the Packers—the *only* player in NFL history to have his jersey retired by two teams. That number stands for a man who believed in giving his all, every single day, in every single thing he did. He showed that real strength isn't just in your muscles but in your heart, in how you treat people, and in how hard you work to make a difference. He crushed quarterbacks on the field, but he also lifted people up everywhere else—teammates, fans, kids, entire communities. Here's the truth Reggie lived by: greatness starts with what you give, not what you take. Play hard. Dream big. Be kind. Lift others. And most importantly, never stop believing that you're here to do something incredible. That's Reggie's story. AND IT CAN BE YOURS TOO.

Joe Montana

THE CALM MIND BEHIND THE GAME'S GREATEST DRIVES

It begins with hands. Joe Montana's hands, small at first, gripping a football too big for him. His dad's hands, calloused from work, guiding his grip, adjusting his throw. His grandmother's hands, flour-dusted and steady, pressing dough into perfect circles for ravioli at the kitchen table while muttering half-prayers in Italian. For a kid growing up in Monongahela, Pennsylvania, hands told the story. They built things, threw things, and, if you were Joe Montana, they pointed toward the future. "Keep your wrist loose, Joey," his dad would say. "You're not throwing a rock at the river; you're throwing art."

Little Joe is born on June 11, 1956 into a family of dreamers and doers. His great-grandfather, Guiseppi Montani, leaves Italy behind in the late 1800s with nothing but his name and a wild hope. He sails across the ocean, trades the Montani "i" for an "a," and sets roots in the US, in a place where the air smells like coal and hard work is a lifestyle. Joe's family works in the steel mills and coal mines—hard hats, dirty hands, and big dreams. Guiseppi's courage to start over plants the seeds of ambition deep in the family tree.

Joe's grandparents speak Italian at home, rolling their R's as they tell him stories about the old country while flour dusts the kitchen air. His grandmother is a champion ravioli-maker, and Joe's childhood memories smell like bubbling marinara sauce and fresh bread baking in the oven. Joe, meanwhile, isn't learning Italian—he's too busy running around and playing tag. Later in life, he says, "I wish I'd learned the language, but when you're a kid, all you care about is if your pants look clean for school." Joe's mom, Theresa, stays up late bleaching his football pants so he's the sharpest kid on the field every week. That kind of effort runs in the family.

Growing up in Monongahela, Joe is surrounded by coal-black hills and Friday night lights. From age 4, he's the kind of kid who can't sit still. He plays everything: baseball, basketball, and, of course, football. Basketball is his first love. His jump shot is smooth, and when he dribbles down the court, his friends can't catch him. He spends hours shooting hoops in the driveway until the sun dips behind the hills and the streetlights buzz to life. Joe plays, eats, sleeps, and breathes sports. But little does he know, his football story is about to steal the spotlight.

In 1964, Joe's dad, Joe Sr., signs him up for youth football a year early by fibbing about his age. The coach squints at the application. "He's nine?" the coach asks, looking at little Joe, who barely reaches the table. Joe Sr. grins. "Big nine," he says, and that's how Joe's football career begins. "My dad wanted me on that field," Joe later says. "And once I got there, I didn't want to leave." Even at eight (or "big nine"), Joe shows that calm-under-pressure coolness that'll later earn him the nickname "Joe Cool." While other kids are fumbling the ball, he's already throwing spiral passes.

By the time Joe is a teenager, he's a local legend. He's the kid who never seems to miss a shot, whether it's a basketball or a football. By 17, he leads his Ringgold High School basketball team to the WPIAL Class AAA championship. Imagine this: packed bleachers, parents shouting like it's a Broadway performance, and Joe coolly dribbling past defenders before sinking a game-winning jumper. He earns all-state honors and even gets a scholarship offer from North Carolina State to play basketball. But something in him whispers, Stick with football.

Joe's high school football career is a different level of drama. He starts playing quarterback at age 16, a position so high-pressure it might as well come with a warning label. The Ringgold High School Rams are his team, and he's their leader. One Friday night, they face Monessen High, the biggest rivals in the county. Joe is on fire, throwing for 223 yards and scoring four touchdowns. A Notre Dame scout sitting in the stands scribbles furiously in his notebook. Later, when people ask him what caught his attention, the scout says, "The kid was magic. Like Houdini in shoulder pads."

But not everyone is a Joe Montana fan. His high school coach, Chuck Abramski, gives Joe a hard time. Abramski doesn't like that Joe plays basketball in the off-season instead of joining his football workouts. When Joe refuses to quit basketball, Abramski benches him for three games. Joe's dad storms into the coach's office, but Joe handles it with quiet determination. When he finally gets back on the field, he plays like a kid with something to prove, slinging touchdowns like frisbees at a summer barbecue. By the end of his senior year, Joe earns a spot as a Parade All-American, one of the highest honors a high school player can get.

Joe's dad is his loudest cheerleader and his toughest coach—a one-man pep squad with a cannon for an arm. Joe Sr. turns their front lawn into a battlefield, firing footballs so fast they leave Joe's hands tingling. "If you can catch my passes," his dad says with a grin, "you can catch anybody's." And just like that, it clicks. Joe's hands turn into superglue, his reflexes sharper than a cat chasing a laser. But the real magic? His dad's life lessons. "The best quarterbacks don't panic," Joe Sr. reminds him. "They think." For Joe, this becomes more than advice—it's his superpower, one he carries all the way to the big leagues.

At home, life slows down, shifting from football drills to family traditions. The Montanas are a tight-knit Italian family. Sunday dinners are sacred. Joe's mom makes enough pasta to feed the whole neighborhood, and the dining table groans under the weight of meatballs, breadsticks, and bowls of salad. Joe's cousins crowd around, passing plates and cracking jokes. Joe sits at the head of the table with sauce on his chin and a smile on his face.

Years later, he'll recreate these meals with his own family, proving that some traditions are too good to let go.

By the time Joe graduates from Ringgold High in 1974, he's a local hero with a future as wide open as a deep pass. Basketball or football? North Carolina State or Notre Dame? The buzz around his basketball skills hints at March Madness dreams, but his football arm? That's pure NFL material. Then, like a game-winning play in the final seconds, Notre Dame steps in with a scholarship to play quarterback. Joe says yes with a grin so wide it could light up the stadium. This decision is bigger than football—it's about stepping into the spotlight of college sports, where legends are made and dreams take flight, where every throw, every play, is a shot at greatness. And if Joe Montana is one thing, it's ready for the big moments.

Before he heads off to South Bend, Indiana, Joe stands in his room. His eyes trace the photos and trophies lining the shelves—snapshots of games won, moments frozen in time. Each tells a story, a step on the ladder to something bigger. His dad walks in, his presence filling the room. With a firm clap on Joe's shoulder, he says, "You're ready, kid." Joe feels the weight of those words, like a handoff of all the lessons, love, and hard work that got him here. He packs his bags carefully, each item a piece of home. Before stepping out, he kisses his mom goodbye, her tearful smile a mix of pride and the ache of letting go. But Joe doesn't leave without a final act of gratitude. He scribbles a note for his coach, Chuck Abramski, and places it where it'll be found: "Thanks for the motivation." Then, he steps onto the road that leads to Notre Dame, the NFL, and the dreams waiting beyond.

Joe Montana arrives at Notre Dame as an 18-year-old with a duffel bag and a dream. The Golden Dome gleams in the Indiana sun, and the buzz around campus is electric. Notre Dame is football royalty, where legends like Knute Rockne and "The Four Horsemen" loom as large as the statues scattered across campus. But when Joe steps onto the freshman team, he isn't treated like a prince. Back then, NCAA rules don't allow freshmen to play varsity, so he spends his first season practicing, studying, and watching from the stands.

He's not a starter yet, but he keeps his head down, learning the playbook like it's his favorite bedtime story.

For most kids, stepping into a program like Notre Dame might be intimidating. But not Joe. He's got the same unflappable calm that he had when he faced down his high school coach, Chuck Abramski. When Joe Sr. taught him how to throw a football, he made it an art. It was about staying cool under pressure and turning every throw into a statement of confidence. "Don't sweat the small stuff," Joe Sr. always said. "Think two steps ahead." Joe keeps this advice in his back pocket like a lucky charm. And he's going to need it because Notre Dame doesn't roll out the red carpet for underdogs.

By his sophomore year, Joe gets his first chance to step onto the varsity field. He doesn't start the season as the top quarterback, but when Notre Dame needs a miracle, they always seem to turn to Joe. Take the game against North Carolina. Notre Dame is trailing late in the fourth quarter, and the crowd in South Bend is already grumbling. Joe trots onto the field, and with the poise of a kid playing catch in his backyard, he leads the team on a game-winning drive. The fans explode in cheers. Later, against Air Force, he does it again, pulling off another stunning comeback. Reporters start whispering about his knack for "magic moments," but Joe shrugs it off. "I just play," he says.

His calm demeanor hides the fact that he's constantly fighting for his spot on the team. Notre Dame's head coach, Dan Devine, isn't entirely sold on Joe. Devine prefers quarterbacks who fit the textbook mold—big, strong, and flashy. Joe is lean, quiet, and methodical. It doesn't help that during his junior year, Joe suffers a shoulder injury that sidelines him for the entire season. The team gives him a medical redshirt, which means he gets an extra year of eligibility, but Joe is frustrated. Sitting out feels like being benched all over again. Still, he doesn't complain. Instead, he uses the time to study the game. He watches film, takes mental reps during practice, and vows to come back stronger.

And come back he does. A few months later, Joe finally gets his shot as Notre Dame's starting quarterback. The year is 1977, a make-or-break moment for the team. Joe knows the stakes and steps up with a quiet resolve to make it count. Early in the season, one game sets the stage for his extraordinary rise. Notre Dame is down against Purdue, and the offense looks lost. The crowd is groaning, and Coach Devine, desperate for answers, turns to Joe. With ice in his veins, Joe steps onto the field and orchestrates a jaw-dropping comeback. He throws touchdown after touchdown, picking apart the defense like it's a math problem he solved in his sleep. By the end of the game, the stadium is roaring his name. From that moment on, Joe Montana is the undisputed leader of the Fighting Irish.

That season, Joe leads Notre Dame all the way to the national championship. On New Year's Day, they face off against the heavily favored Texas Longhorns in the Cotton Bowl. The stakes are sky-high, but Joe is as calm as ever. Under his leadership, Notre Dame crushes Texas 38-10, and Joe's performance cements his reputation as a clutch player. The Fighting Irish are national champions, and Joe Montana's legend is officially born. When reporters ask him about the pressure of the big game, Joe grins. "Pressure? That's just football," he says.

From late-night study sessions to grueling practice drills, Joe's college years became a proving ground where every setback fueled his determination. The journey was filled with sharp turns and uphill climbs, it was here he learned to turn obstacles into stepping stones toward greatness. Each moment tested his resolve and pushed his limits to new heights. The following season, in 1978, he plays in what becomes one of the most famous games of his life: the "Chicken Soup Game." It's the Cotton Bowl again, this time against Houston, and the conditions are brutal. The temperature in Dallas is below freezing, with an icy wind that cuts through the stadium like a knife. Players are shivering on the sidelines, and fans are bundled up like they're at the North Pole. Joe, however, is more than just cold—he's sick. Really sick. He's been battling the flu all week, and by halftime, his body gives out. The team doctors find him in the locker room, shaking all over and so cold that his body was starting to shut down.

"Joe's done," they tell Coach Devine. But Joe isn't done. Wrapped in blankets, sipping chicken soup to warm up, he somehow finds the strength to go back out for the second half. What happens next feels like a scene from a blockbuster movie. Notre Dame is down 34-12, and hope seems like a distant memory. The stadium feels frozen in more ways than one, with fans bundled tight and silence hanging heavy in the air. Then Joe steps onto the field, his face pale and his breath visible in the frigid air. He looks more like a warrior braving his final stand than a quarterback in a football game. Snap after snap, he carves through Houston's defense, his passes sharp and unyielding, like arrows piercing through enemy lines. The crowd begins to stir, first with murmurs and then with roars, as touchdown after touchdown narrows the gap. With just seconds on the clock, Joe takes the snap, scans the field, and delivers a perfect pass into the end zone. The crowd erupts in disbelief and pure joy. Notre Dame has won 35-34, etching this game into the annals of college football history as one of the most extraordinary comebacks ever seen. Years later, Joe reflects on that game with his trademark humor: "That soup was really good."

By the time Joe graduates with a degree in business administration, he's a household name in college football. Notre Dame fans worship him like a hero from a Greek myth, and NFL scouts are circling like hawks. Joe's genius lies in how he transforms every play into a vivid display of strategy, skill, and unshakable focus. He stays cool when others crumble. He turns impossible situations into unforgettable moments. He's not the flashiest quarterback or the strongest, but he's the one you want when the game is on the line. As Joe himself puts it, "I don't care if it's two minutes or twenty. If there's time on the clock, there's a way to win."

As Joe packs his bags and says goodbye to South Bend, he carries with him the lessons of his Notre Dame years: resilience, determination, and an uncanny ability to stay calm under fire. He doesn't know it yet, but his greatest challenges—and his greatest triumphs—are still ahead. For now, he's a kid from Monongahela with four Super Bowl rings still waiting for him in the future.

Joe Montana's NFL story begins like a quiet storm. Somewhere around 1979, after a college career marked by miraculous comebacks, he's drafted by the San Francisco 49ers in the third round, 82nd overall. The draft analysts barely blinked—third round? For a guy like Joe? It seems some NFL scouts were still underestimating his knack for pulling magic out of thin air. But Joe brushes it off. "The round doesn't matter," he says. "I'm here now. That's what matters." When he arrives in San Francisco as a 23-year-old rookie, he's wide-eyed and eager, soaking in the experience. His first season isn't dazzling—he spends most of it on the bench—but Joe uses the time wisely, quietly preparing, watching, and waiting. He's plotting his rise.

By his second NFL season, Joe starts showing everyone what Notre Dame fans already know: this guy is clutch. His first major NFL moment comes against the New Orleans Saints. The 49ers are down 35-7 at halftime. The game looks done. Fans are already heading for the exits, Joe calmly walks into the huddle and tells his teammates, "We're not losing this one." What follows is a comeback so outrageous it could only come from Joe

Cool. He throws two sharp, spiraling touchdowns, scrambles with a determination that electrifies the crowd, and orchestrates the team's victory—a heart-pounding 38-35 win. Each play seems infused with a kind of gritty magic, as if Joe is painting a masterpiece on the field, one bold stroke at a time. It's the biggest comeback in NFL history at the time. "That was the moment we all realized he was different," says Hall of Famer Ronnie Lott. "Joe wasn't just playing football. He was rewriting the rules."

In 1981, Joe becomes the starting quarterback, and it's off to the races. That season, the 49ers go 13-3 and make it all the way to the NFC Championship Game against the Dallas Cowboys. With 58 seconds left, Joe and the 49ers trail 27-21. On 3rd-and-3, Joe takes the snap and rolls to his right. Defensive linemen are chasing him like angry bulls. He keeps his cool, pump fakes, and fires a high pass to the corner of the end zone. Dwight Clark leaps into the air and snags the ball with his fingertips. The play—forever immortalized as "The Catch"—becomes one of the most famous moments in NFL history. The 49ers win the game, go to their first Super Bowl, and beat the Cincinnati Bengals. Joe Montana is named Super Bowl MVP. He's 25 years old.

The next few years turn Joe into a football superstar, a name every fan knows and admires. In 1984, he takes the 49ers on an amazing run, winning 15 out of 16 games in the regular season. They finish it off with a big Super Bowl win, beating the Miami Dolphins 38-16. Joe picks apart defenses like he's solving crossword puzzles. "It's like watching a surgeon work," says one teammate.

After years of dazzling the league with his brilliance, the grind of football starts to leave its mark on Joe. His body, once seemingly untouchable, begins to feel the weight of all those bone-crushing tackles and high-stakes moments. By 1986, the wear and tear catches up with Joe in a big way. A crushing hit leaves him with a back injury, and doctors warn his career might be over. For most players, that would be the end of the story. Joe, refusing to back down, pours his energy into recovery and stages a remarkable comeback, earning the NFL Comeback Player of the Year award. It's a moment that redefines his resilience and sets the stage for his next chapter.

By 1988, Joe is back in peak form. That year's Super Bowl is unforgettable: he leads a 92-yard game-winning drive in the final three minutes to beat the Bengals. On the sidelines, he famously points out actor John Candy in the stands to calm his teammates. "We all wanted to panic," Ronnie Lott recalls. "Joe wanted to talk about snacks." Then, one year later, Joe's Super Bowl performance will be a masterclass in precision and brilliance. He throws five touchdowns and racks up 297 yards in a 55-10 demolition of the Denver Broncos. He wins his third Super Bowl MVP, and by this point, people aren't just calling him great—they're calling him the greatest of all time. The GOAT.

Not long after his triumphant 1989 Super Bowl performance, the cracks in Joe's armor start to show. By 1991, an elbow injury sidelines him for almost two full seasons, leaving him watching from the sidelines as the 49ers reshape their team. When Joe finally returns to the field in 1992, he finds that the franchise has moved on, placing their future in the hands of Steve Young. For Joe, who had spent his career battling to prove himself, the decision feels like a gut punch. "I didn't understand it," he admits. "I just wanted a chance to compete."

In 1993, Joe gets traded to the Kansas City Chiefs. At 37, many people think he's washed up. But Joe being Joe, he's not ready to fade away quietly yet. In his first season with the Chiefs, he leads them to their first AFC Championship Game since 1970. Along the way, he pulls off more vintage Montana magic, including a stunning last-minute drive to beat John Elway's Denver Broncos. Even in his late 30s, Joe proves he still has ice water in his veins. He plays one more season before announcing his retirement at age 38.

When he hangs up his cleats, Joe Montana's resume sparkles: four Super Bowl championships, three Super Bowl MVPs, and a reputation as the ultimate clutch player. The 49ers retire his No. 16 jersey in 1997, and in 2000, he's inducted into the Pro Football Hall of Fame. By then, the nickname "Joe Cool" wasn't just about staying calm during tough moments—it was about being the guy who made the impossible look easy, a player whose game-winning drives became stories kids would tell on playgrounds for years to come.

After football, Joe has to figure out who he is without the game. At first, he struggles. He tries broadcasting, but it's not a great fit. He dabbles in business ventures, some of which succeed, and some of which flop. "Retirement was hard," says his wife, Jennifer. "Football gave him a purpose. He needed to find a new one."

What brings Joe the most joy during this time is his family. He and Jennifer, who met on the set of a razor commercial, have four kids: Alexandra, Elizabeth, Nate, and Nick. As much as Joe loves football, he loves being a dad even more. He attends their games, teaches them life lessons, and hosts big Sunday dinners where everyone gathers around the table. The Montana household is like something out of an Italian sitcom. There's pasta, laughter, and enough teasing to keep everyone humble. "We're very Italian," Jennifer says. "A lot of eating, a lot of cooking, a lot of yelling. It's chaos, but it's beautiful."

One of Joe's favorite post-football hobbies is cooking. And he's serious about it. His wood-fired pizza oven is the centerpiece of family gatherings. Joe kneads dough like he's throwing a football, with focus and precision. His pizzas are legendary, topped with fresh basil, mozzarella, and a little bit of magic. "I've got my nonna's sauce recipe," Joe brags. "But don't ask for it. It's a family secret."

In retirement, Joe also discovers a love for travel. He and Jennifer explore the world, from the canals of Venice to the beaches of Costa Rica. They hike Machu Picchu with their kids, surf in Hawaii, and sail through the Mediterranean. Joe was soaking up moments. "It's about being with the people you love," he says. "That's what matters."

As Joe ages, he finds peace in the little things: his grandchildren calling him "Yogi," Sunday barbecues on the terrace, and nights spent playing dominos with Jennifer. He still feels the aches and pains from his football days—he's had over two dozen surgeries—but he doesn't let that define him. "Would I do it all again?" he says. "Absolutely. Every hit. Every throw. Every win. It was worth it."

These days, Joe splits his time between San Francisco and Napa Valley, where he produces wine and supports charities like the Make-A-Wish Foundation. When he's not working, he's spending time with his growing family. "Life's good," Joe says with a smile. "It's not about the trophies anymore. It's about the people."

And so, the kid from Monongahela who once dreamed of throwing touchdowns and making a difference has done both. Joe Montana, the GOAT, the family man, the pizza master, has found his ultimate end zone: happiness.

Amazing Facts, Records, and Moments

Origins and Early Evolution

Rugby's Wild Child

Before the super-popular American football we know today took the spotlight, it was just a wild, rowdy kid breaking away from rugby's rules! Back in the mid-1800s, college students in America couldn't agree on how to play. At Harvard, they'd grab the ball and run like crazy! At Yale, they'd kick, kick, kick! And at Princeton, they mixed in some soccer moves. Every school had its own ideas, and the big challenge before matches was deciding which set of rules to follow—sometimes that took longer than playing the game! All this chaos and creativity led to something brand-new and totally American. **Takeaway:** From this wild mix of running, kicking, and arguing, American football eventually found its own identity!

The 1869 Rutgers-Princeton Showdown

The very first official college football match happened way back on November 6, 1869, when Rutgers and Princeton faced off. Don't think modern touchdowns and helmets—this was more like a bouncy, rough blend of soccer and rugby. Players couldn't even carry the ball; they had to kick it, whack it with their hands, or even use their heads! Rutgers won 6-4 and crowned themselves champs, proving that Americans loved this lively, contact-filled clash—even if the rules were still a bit wacky. **Takeaway:** The 1869 Rutgers-Princeton game lit the spark that set American football on its incredible journey!

Harvard's Revolutionary Visitors

In 1874, Harvard invited Canada's McGill University onto their field—and got a surprise that changed the game forever. The Canadian players showed off rugby-style rules that let you *carry* the ball. Harvard was hooked! They blended this clever idea with their own "Boston Game" tricks, launching American football toward its bold new style. Suddenly, charging forward with the ball became part of the fun. **Takeaway:** That showdown helped give American football one of its coolest moves—running with the ball!

Rules Bring Order (Sort Of)

By 1876, players and fans were tired of arguing over rules. To clean up the chaos, colleges formed the Intercollegiate Football Association and wrote a real rulebook! Sure, the rules still looked a lot like rugby, but at least everyone was (mostly) on the same page now. As time passed, these new guidelines nudged the sport away from its earlier madness and toward a smarter, more organized game. **Takeaway:** Early efforts to create official rules turned wild brawls into a game with structure and strategy.

The Brutality of Early Football

In the late 1800s, stepping onto a football field was like charging into battle! No helmets, no pads—just players clobbering each other like human battering rams. Broken bones and bloody noses were common, and some schools even tried to ban the game. One legendary match left half the players too hurt to keep going! But this bone-crunching start forced football to get safer gear and smarter plays, making it a better game for everyone. **Takeaway:** Early football was super rough, but that roughness pushed the sport to protect players and evolve into what we know today.

Why the Ball Changed Shape

Imagine playing with a round ball made from a pig's bladder—yuck! That's what early footballs were like. Eventually, players realized an oval shape was easier to grip, pass, and carry. By the late 1800s, the familiar pointed football took over. This new shape helped the game move faster and added tons of excitement every time someone ran down the field with it. **Takeaway:** Switching to a sleek, oval ball kicked football's speed and style into high gear.

College Fans Go Wild

By the 1880s, football wasn't just a game—it was a full-throttle campus party! Students held pep rallies, played in marching bands, and shouted catchy cheers. People wore their school colors proudly, waved giant banners, and turned the field into a place of nonstop excitement. Over time, these early gatherings would grow into the tailgating parties and halftime shows we love today. **Takeaway:** College football fun reached beyond the field, pumping up fans and building the traditions we still celebrate!

Walter Camp's Genius Invention

In the 1880s, Yale's Walter Camp—known as the "Father of American Football"—had a game-changing idea: the line of scrimmage. Instead of everyone piling into a jumble like in rugby, teams now faced off neatly, planning tricky plays and strategies. Thinking fast and outsmarting your opponent suddenly mattered as much as strength. This genius tweak turned football into the clever, action-packed sport we cheer for now. **Takeaway:** Walter Camp's brilliant twist brought order and brainpower into football, making it a smarter, more exciting showdown.

The Rise of the Touchdown

At first, kicking the ball through goalposts was a big deal. But as American football grew, carrying the ball into the end zone became the star of the show—the touchdown! What started as a single point grew in value and glory. Soon, sprinting for that end zone and scoring a touchdown was the ultimate thrill, putting speedy runs and daring passes at the heart of the game. **Takeaway:** Touchdowns turned American football into a daring race toward the goal line, lighting up the scoreboard and our excitement.

An All-American Identity Emerges

By the late 19th century, American football had shaken off most of its rugby roots. With a unique set of rules, a distinctive ball shape, clever strategies, and fast-paced action, the sport became something proudly American. With its very own rules, look, and style, football rose as a one-of-a-kind American pastime—bold, brilliant, and beloved!

The Field, Ball, and Stadiums

A Super-Sized Green "Stage"

Stretching 360 feet long (120 yards, including the two 10-yard end zones) and 160 feet wide (53⅓ yards), a football field is a massive green canvas where epic moments unfold. Trimmed to precise perfection, it's the ultimate stage for players to clash, strategize, and dazzle under the spotlight. Whether it's natural grass groomed like a fancy golf course fairway or high-tech synthetic turf crafted to stay smooth and green, this colossal surface is a super-sized stage for big-time action. The outer boundary lines, painted to razor-sharp perfection, frame the "rug" on which everyone competes. **Takeaway:** The field's generous dimensions and precisely marked edges ensure a fair, flat surface, setting the perfect scene for spectacular moments.

Yard Lines—The Field's Built-In Rulers

Peek at a football field and you'll see crisp white lines crossing it every five yards, along with numbers every 10 yards. Smaller "hash marks" sit near the center, showing exactly where the ball should be placed. It's like the field has its own ruler and compass, ensuring no one ever doubts their exact spot. These lines form a finely organized grid so coaches, players, and fans can measure every foot of progress. **Takeaway:** These interior yard lines and marks turn the field into a giant measuring tool, making sure everyone knows exactly where the action unfolds.

End Zones—Colorful Finish Lines and Goal Posts—Sky-High Targets

At each end of the field lies a special 10-yard zone often bursting with bright colors—these are the end zones, like big welcoming arms ready to hug the ball. Above them, tall goal posts stretch into the sky, with the crossbar set 10 feet high and the uprights 18 feet 6 inches apart. These structures proudly announce: "Score here!" or "Aim your kick between these posts!" **Takeaway:** Visible finish lines and towering posts clearly mark scoring zones, making it easy to see where big points are earned.

Grass or Turf—The Field's Fancy Carpet

Some fields use natural grass so perfect it's like a storybook meadow, while others rely on cutting-edge synthetic turf that mimics real blades. Underneath, drainage systems whisk away rain so the surface stays firm and safe. Whether it's nature's green masterpiece or a scientific wonder, the goal is a smooth, stable playing field ready for action in any weather. **Takeaway:** By choosing the right surface, the field remains clean, comfy, and consistently playable, rain or shine.

The Football's Funny Shape—A Fast-Flying Oddball

Hold a football next to a soccer ball and you'll grin—one's round as a bubble and the other's shaped like a pointy egg! Officially known as a prolate spheroid, it measures about 11 inches tip to tip and about 21 inches around at its widest, helping it slice through the air. When thrown in a perfect spiral, it speeds like a mini missile. **Takeaway:** Its unusual shape isn't just quirky—it's tuned for long, steady flight, making passes zip through the sky with precision.

Leather, Laces, and Grippy Goodness

A modern football is made of top-quality leather, its surface speckled with tiny "pebbles" for a better grip. The white laces stitched along one side aren't just decoration—they're a sturdy hold for passing. Pick it up and feel how it nestles in your hand, crafted for ultimate control. **Takeaway:** These details help players handle the ball skillfully, ensuring top-notch throws and confident catches.

Perfect Weight and Bounce—No Over-Inflated Egos Here!

A football weighs about as much as your favorite water bottle (14 to 15 ounces) and is pumped just right to feel firm but still a little squishy (12.5 to 13.5 psi). This perfect balance makes it springy enough to zip through the air and bounce just right when it lands. If it's too soft, it'll flop; too hard, and it'll be a wild cannonball! **Takeaway:** The ball's precise weight and pressure create predictable, skill-based gameplay, making every pass, kick, and catch feel "just right."

Stadium Seating—Your Own Personal View of the Show

A football stadium often seats tens of thousands of fans in rows that curve around the field like a colossal bowl. Each seat is angled to catch all the action, with some stadiums holding crowds larger than entire towns! Thoughtfully planned aisles and sightlines make everyone feel close to the spectacle. **Takeaway:** Smart seating design ensures that, whether you're near the field or high above, you'll see the game unfold clearly and feel part of the fun.

Domes and Retractable Roofs—Weather Wizards

Some stadiums have giant, special roofs that act like umbrellas for the whole field. When the sun is shining, they slide open to let in the light. If it's raining or snowing, they close up tight, keeping everyone inside dry and cozy. These roofs make sure games can go on, no matter what's happening outside! **Takeaway:** Controlled environments keep fans comfortable and the field in top shape, ensuring weather never dampens the excitement.

Mega Screens and Surround Sound—A Superhero Cinema Experience

Modern stadiums boast giant high-definition video boards—sometimes over 100 feet wide—showing replays, stats, and dazzling animations. Surround-sound speakers bring every pad-crunching tackle and crowd roar to your ears in vivid detail. It's like watching sports in a futuristic theater! **Takeaway:** Huge screens and crystal-clear audio immerse fans completely, making the stadium feel like a high-energy entertainment epicenter.

Rules and Gameplay

Downs—Four Tries to Move the Chains

In modern American football, the offense always faces a ticking challenge: advance the ball at least 10 yards within four attempts called "downs." Think of it like climbing a 10-yard ladder in four steps! If they make it, the officials wave their arms for a fresh "first down," and the offense gets another four tries to keep marching forward. If not, the other team takes over on offense. It's a never-ending tug-of-war of distance, where every yard gained can feel like winning a tiny treasure. **Takeaway**: Downs matter because they're the engine that keeps the game roaring ahead.

Touchdowns—The Six-Point Sprint to Glory

A touchdown is the crown jewel of scoring. The offense must get the football into the opposing team's end zone—running it across the goal line or catching it there—securing possession for a fat six points. It's like finding buried gold at the end of a hard-fought journey! Touchdowns reward teamwork, clever planning, and bold moves. The whole stadium erupts in cheers because this is the big score everyone chases. **Takeaway**: Touchdowns reward determination and teamwork. They remind us that bold efforts can unlock the greatest rewards.

Extra Points and Two-Point Conversions—Tiny Kicks or Daring Dashes

Right after a touchdown, the offense gets a crack at bonus points. Usually, they'll try a quick kick called an "extra point" for one additional score. But if they crave even more excitement, they can attempt a "two-point conversion" by running or passing the ball over the same goal line again. This riskier choice, if successful, doubles the bonus. **Takeaway**: Extra points and conversions let teams add a clever twist to their scoring. They teach us that sometimes playing it safe is good, but taking a calculated risk can yield even sweeter rewards.

Field Goals—Three Points of Laser-Like Accuracy

If the offense can't reach the end zone, they can still salvage their drive by aiming for a field goal. A player kicks the ball through tall yellow uprights, earning three points if it soars straight and true. It's like threading a needle with your foot—precision rules! Field goals turn near-misses into valuable points, keeping the scoreboard ticking even when the offense stalls. **Takeaway**: Field goals matter because they show that not every plan ends perfectly, but careful skill and steady nerves can still bring victory in smaller doses.

Safeties—Defense's Surprise Two-Point Strike

When an offense ends up pinned deep in its own scoring area and the defense tackles them there, it's called a "safety." This earns the defense two points, like snagging secret bonus coins right from under the offense's nose! Plus, the offense must kick the ball away to the defense after this happens. It's a sudden shift that can change the game in a snap. **Takeaway**: Safeties show that strong defense can flip the script fast. They teach us that in football (and life), staying alert and pouncing at the right moment can pay off big-time.

The Clock—Four Quarters of Ticking Tension

A standard American football game runs for four quarters, each 15 minutes long—totaling 60 minutes of game time. But the clock doesn't just roll on silently; it stops for incomplete passes, players running out of bounds, and other special moments. This means time management is crucial. Teams must move quickly when they're behind or use the clock like a shield to protect a lead. The clock is a secret partner or enemy—depending on how you handle it! **Takeaway**: The clock shapes strategy. It reminds us that every second counts and that smart planning and quick action can mean the difference between losing and winning.

Kickoffs—Launching the Action High and Far

At the start of the game and right after anyone scores, a kickoff sends the ball sailing through the air from one team to the other. Imagine pressing a big "reset" button: new possession, fresh start, let the adventure continue! The receiving team tries to run the ball forward before their offense takes over and tries to score again. **Takeaway**: Kickoffs reset the stage. They teach us that every new beginning gives a fresh chance to shine, no matter what happened before.

Penalties—Yellow Flags for Playing Nice and Fair

If a player breaks a rule—maybe by blocking someone unfairly or interfering with a pass—an official chucks a bright yellow flag onto the field. This penalty often means losing yards or canceling a dazzling play that just happened. It's like getting a "redo" but with a big disadvantage! Penalties keep everyone honest, respectful, and on their best behavior. **Takeaway**: Penalties safeguard fairness. They remind us that rules aren't made to spoil the fun, but to keep the game safe, respectful, and balanced.

Challenges and Reviews—Turning Back the Clock on Mistakes

Coaches hold a secret weapon: the challenge flag. If they suspect the officials made a mistake, they can toss this red flag to trigger a slow-motion video review. If the replay proves the call was wrong, the officials correct it. It's like having a magical "instant replay time machine" to ensure the truth shines through. **Takeaway**: Challenges guarantee honesty and accuracy. They teach us that double-checking important decisions can prevent unfair outcomes.

Overtime—When the Game Usually Doesn't End in a Tie

If both teams remain perfectly even when the clock runs out, the game enters a special overtime period. Different leagues have different overtime rules, but the idea is simple: give both teams a fair shot to break the tie and claim victory. It's like adding extra innings in baseball or a tie-breaker in a video game—except the stakes are sky-high, and the tension is electric! **Takeaway**: Overtime usually ensures there's a winner, teaching us that when regular time isn't enough, we sometimes need a fair and final showdown to settle the score.

Roles on the Field

Quarterbacks: The Brainy Play-Callers

Quarterbacks are the team's top decision-makers, guiding every offensive snap like master chess players who see the whole board. Before the ball even moves, they carefully study the defense, choose the best play to attack it, and then use hand signals or special code words to alert their teammates. Once the action starts, they throw lightning-fast passes, hand off the ball to a runner, or even run forward themselves if they spot an opening. **Takeaway:** Quarterbacks show us that thinking quickly and leading with confidence can turn smart plans into game-changing results.

Running Backs: The Speedy Ball-Carriers

Running backs zoom ahead with the football tucked securely under their arm, weaving through defenders like race cars zipping around traffic cones. They're known for their explosive starts, quick cuts, and toughness when crashing through crowded spaces. They don't just run, though—some running backs block defenders to help protect their teammates or catch short passes to keep the offense rolling. **Takeaway:** Running backs remind us that charging forward fearlessly—and sometimes clearing a path for others—can transform tough situations into big gains.

Wide Receivers: The Super-Fast Catchers

Wide receivers blaze downfield at top speed, spinning and leaping to grab passes right out of midair. They're experts at running precise routes—like secret pathways—tricking defenders into going the wrong way. With quick footwork and sticky hands, they often turn a good throw into a jaw-dropping highlight. **Takeaway:** Wide receivers teach us that practice, perfect timing, and staying focused can help us catch opportunities and shine brightly.

Tight Ends: The Mighty Hybrids

Tight ends are built like tough trucks but move with surprising grace. One moment, they're slamming into defenders to open a lane for the running back; the next, they're sprinting into the open field to catch a pass. This double-duty role demands both muscle and finesse, making them priceless assets on offense. **Takeaway:** Tight ends show us that mixing power with skill can turn you into a versatile teammate who can handle almost any challenge.

Offensive Linemen: The Great Protectors

Offensive linemen form the "Great Wall" that shields their teammates. While they rarely touch the ball, their blocking skills are crucial. They must hold off charging defenders, giving the quarterback time to throw and creating open lanes for the running backs. Without them, the offense wouldn't stand a chance. **Takeaway:** Offensive linemen prove that unseen heroes, who put teamwork first, can make all the difference in reaching your goals.

Defensive Linemen: The Powerful Disrupters

Defensive linemen are like human bulldozers, smashing through the offense's protective wall. Their mission: tackle the running back or pressure the quarterback before the play can fully unfold. They rely on explosive strength, quick reactions, and smart hand-fighting moves to break free from blockers. **Takeaway:** Defensive linemen show that strong determination—combined with force and smarts—can crumble even the toughest barriers.

Linebackers: The Smart and Strong Stoppers

Linebackers are the defense's all-around defenders, standing just behind the linemen. They must react in a split second—rushing forward to tackle a runner, shifting sideways to cover a receiver, or dropping back to guard against a pass. With keen awareness and balanced strength, they're always ready to halt any threat. **Takeaway:** Linebackers remind us that watching carefully, adjusting to what's happening, and acting quickly are keys to protecting what matters most.

Cornerbacks: The Clever Lockdown Artists

Cornerbacks face off against wide receivers, sticking to them like glue to prevent big catches. Using swift footwork and top-notch instincts, they try to read the receiver's moves before the ball arrives. When a pass flies their way, they reach in, jump up, or knock it down—sometimes even snatching it for themselves. **Takeaway:** Cornerbacks teach us that staying close, paying attention, and reacting fast can keep big problems from getting past you.

Safeties: The Eyes in the Backfield

Safeties hang out behind most defenders, watching the entire play unfold like hawks circling overhead. With a great view, they rush in to help stop a run, dart sideways to block a pass, or even swoop in for an interception. Their job calls for quick thinking and fearless action, serving as the final safety net for their team. **Takeaway:** Safeties show us that staying alert, ready, and brave can help you rescue the day when all else fails.

Kickers and Punters: The Precision Launchers

Kickers and punters handle the ball with their feet, delivering mighty boots that send it soaring. Kickers aim between the tall goalposts, scoring points with pinpoint accuracy. Punters launch the ball deep downfield to push opponents far away. Their jobs demand steady nerves, spot-on focus, and a rocket-like leg. **Takeaway:** Kickers and punters prove that calm concentration, careful aim, and a single well-placed strike can have a massive impact on the game's direction.

Leagues Organization

The NFL's Big Family and Its Two Conferences

Right now, the top professional league, the NFL, is like one big family reunion with 32 teams. These teams are split evenly into two big "families" called conferences: the American Football Conference (AFC) and the National Football Conference (NFC). Each conference is then broken down into four mini "neighborhoods" called divisions, each with exactly four teams. This setup makes it easy for fans to know exactly who their team is racing against all year long! **Takeaway:** Seeing how the NFL is neatly organized helps you follow the action, keeping you from feeling lost and making every matchup more fun to track.

Each Team Wears Its City on Its Sleeve

Every NFL team proudly carries the name of the city or region it calls home, making that team a kind of sports ambassador for its area. From the team name to the colors on the players' uniforms, you can spot local pride all over the place. Cities and regions love this bond, and fans feel like they're cheering their hometown spirit. **Takeaway:** Knowing that teams stand for entire communities helps you see that football isn't just about the field—it's also about hometown pride and coming together.

A Season That's One Long Adventure

The NFL season kicks off in early September and rolls on into early January, fitting in 17 games per team over 18 weeks of pure excitement. Each team gets one "bye week" to rest up. This steady march of games feels like a giant puzzle where every piece counts—one surprising upset can shake up the entire playoff picture! **Takeaway:** Understanding the season's length and pace shows that every game is like a stepping stone, pushing teams closer to their ultimate dream: a spot in the playoffs.

The Playoffs: Where Only the Best Survive

After the regular season ends, it's playoff time. The playoffs are a single-elimination showdown, where one loss means you're done. Only the cream of the crop from each conference get in, and from there, it's a roller coaster of heart-stopping games. The pressure is huge, and no one wants to pack up and go home early. **Takeaway:** Appreciating the playoffs helps you understand why players give everything they've got in every game—because the path to the championship is truly a do-or-die adventure.

How Teams Earn a Playoff Spot

Getting into the playoffs isn't just about winning a lot; it's also about outplaying the teams in your division. First, each of the four division champions in a conference earns a seat at the playoff table. Then, three more teams with the best leftover records (called "wild cards") squeeze in. This mix of division winners and wild cards makes the playoff race an unpredictable thrill ride! **Takeaway:** Realizing how teams qualify for the playoffs reminds you that there's more than one way to succeed, and that hanging tough until the very end can make all the difference.

The Draft: Picking Tomorrow's Superstars

The NFL Draft happens every spring and is like a giant player "shopping spree" for teams. The team with the worst record from last season picks first, and the champion picks last. This fairness-focused system helps weaker teams land fresh talent. By sharing top prospects more evenly, the league stays competitive—nobody gets stuck at the bottom forever! **Takeaway:** Understanding the draft order shows that the league is built to keep things balanced, teaching us that in football—and in life—everyone deserves a chance to improve.

Seven Rounds of Talent Treasure Hunting

The Draft isn't just one round; it's seven rounds of serious scouting. Teams dig deep to find hidden gems who might blossom into future stars. Some picks are big names everyone knows, while others are quieter finds that surprise everyone later. This long, careful process shows that you never know where the next standout player will come from! **Takeaway:** Seeing how long and detailed the draft is reminds you that success often grows from patience, strategy, and looking beyond the obvious choices.

Other Leagues That Keep the Gridiron Buzzing

The NFL may be the biggest show, but it's not the only one. There are other pro football leagues—like the XFL and USFL—offering extra games and championships. They often play when the NFL isn't in season, giving fans bonus action to follow, new rules to explore, and a fresh stage for players to shine. **Takeaway:** Knowing about other leagues tells you that football's excitement doesn't stop with the NFL; the sport's world is wide and full of surprises to keep fans cheering year-round.

The Salary Cap: A Financial Fair-Play Tool

The NFL uses a "salary cap," a budget limit that stops teams from piling up too many superstar contracts. By making sure no team can spend endlessly, the league protects competitive balance. It's like a rule that says, "Everyone gets the same toolbox—now build the best team you can!" **Takeaway:** Understanding the salary cap teaches that fairness and creativity beat bottomless wallets, making the competition more honest and intense.

The Hidden Heroes Behind the Scenes

The NFL doesn't run on football players alone. Skilled planners, executives, and organizers work year-round on schedules, events like the draft, and playoff formats to keep the league rolling smoothly. They tackle tough decisions—like which teams play on Monday nights or when the next big championship game will be—to give fans an organized, edge-of-your-seat experience.

Historic Rivalries

Packers vs. Bears – The Timeless Tug-of-War

Imagine two neighbors who have been arguing over the same fence line for more than 100 years! That's what it's like when the Green Bay Packers meet the Chicago Bears. Their very first clash took place in 1921, making their face-offs older than your great-grandpa's photo albums. With over 200 meetings, these two teams have battled through freezing winters and roaring crowds, each game feeling like a living time capsule of football's earliest days. **Takeaway:** This shows how a rivalry can stretch across generations, turning every showdown into a link in a gigantic chain of shared history.

Cowboys vs. Washington – A Holiday Showstopper

Picture a table piled high with turkey and mashed potatoes, and families huddled close around the TV. Now add the Dallas Cowboys and Washington lining up on the field, ready to rumble, and you've got one of the most talked-about rivalries anywhere. These teams have squared off for decades, meeting in fierce contests that sometimes fall on Thanksgiving, making family gatherings even more exciting! Whenever they clash, both sides bring extra spark, as if the day's feast gives fans more energy to cheer—and sometimes argue—over who's the best. **Takeaway:** This shows that a rivalry can turn an ordinary holiday afternoon into a heart-pounding memory shared by people all across the country.

Steelers vs. Ravens – The Storm of the Century

When the Pittsburgh Steelers charge onto the field to face the Baltimore Ravens, it's like thunder and lightning colliding in the sky. Since the late 1990s, these matchups have been nail-biters, often decided by a slim margin. Fans know that every single second counts, with leads vanishing into thin air and late-game surprises common. Think of two thunderclouds smashing together in a wild storm—nobody's sure which one will produce the final, mighty boom. **Takeaway:** This shows how fierce competition can turn a regular meeting into a pressure-packed adventure where anything can happen right up until the clock hits zero.

Giants vs. Eagles – Big City Sparks Fly

Two East Coast neighbors, separated by a short drive and divided by a river of fierce loyalty, set the stage for a rivalry that's been thrilling fans for decades. That's what happens when the New York Giants meet the Philadelphia Eagles. Their battles date back to 1933 and are famous for wild surprises, such as the "Miracle at the Meadowlands" in 1978, when a last-second twist left fans gasping in disbelief. Every showdown feels like riding a super-fast roller coaster: thrilling loops, sudden drops, and a heart-pounding finish. **Takeaway:** This shows that rivalries can create legendary moments so astonishing that fans remember them for decades, passing the story down like a treasured family tale.

Raiders vs. Chiefs – Desert Grit and City Pride

Step into the late 1960s and '70s, and you'll find two teams battling under the hot sun, where swirling dust and echoing cheers set the stage for the Las Vegas (formerly Oakland) Raiders against the Kansas City Chiefs. Back then, their clashes were so intense that spectators held their breath, fearing to miss a single blow of this epic tug-of-war. These matchups often tipped the balance of an entire season, each winner leaving the field as if they'd just won a gold nugget in a high-noon showdown. **Takeaway:** This matters because it shows how a rivalry can feel like a gritty, old Western, turning ordinary games into high-stakes duels that echo through history.

49ers vs. Cowboys – High-Flying Showdowns

When the San Francisco 49ers cross paths with the Dallas Cowboys, it's like two champion acrobats trying to out-do each other with the most spectacular flips and twists. During the 1970s and again in the 1990s, their matchups often decided who would march on toward the year's top prize. One unforgettable game in the early 1980s included a last-gasp catch so stunning it's still replayed and talked about today. Fans tuned in knowing they might witness fireworks that could shape the entire season's story. **Takeaway:** This shows that timing and high stakes can transform a rivalry into a legendary spectacle, making a single game echo in fans' minds for ages.

Army vs. Navy – A Game of Honor

Picture a grand scene filled with marching bands, proud uniforms, and a stadium brimming with excitement. That's the atmosphere whenever Army faces Navy, a rivalry that started in 1890 and has been played nearly every year since. This matchup is a celebration of tradition, loyalty, and the values these schools represent. Thousands gather, not just as fans, but as people who respect the history and meaning behind every tackle and cheer. **Takeaway:** This shows that a rivalry can stand for something bigger than just a scoreboard, shining like a beacon of honor and pride for everyone watching.

Ohio State vs. Michigan – "The Game" That Splits Friendships

Since 1897, this showdown has sparked passionate debates in classrooms, playgrounds, and living rooms across the Midwest. Known simply as "The Game," it's a rivalry so heated that entire towns split into two colors: one side cheering for Ohio State, the other roaring for Michigan. On some occasions, both teams entered the clash at the absolute top of their form, making it feel like a championship before the championship. When these two collide, fans don't just watch—they hold their breath. **Takeaway:** This shows how a rivalry can become a massive community event, where everyone from grandparents to tiny tots can unite (or divide) behind their chosen side.

USC vs. Notre Dame – A Coast-to-Coast Classic

Stretch a map of the United States from shining West Coast shores to quiet Midwest towns, and you'll find the legendary rivalry between the University of Southern California (USC) and Notre Dame. Starting in 1926, this yearly face-off pulls fans from all over the country into a lively tug-of-war of cheers. It's a rare cross-country rivalry where every contest hums with excitement, storied traditions, and booming chants, making it feel like a festive parade of school spirit that never loses its glow.

Record-Breaking Players and Coaches

Jerry Rice's Towering Pile of Receiving Yards

Jerry Rice, a wide receiver known for making even the trickiest catches look easy, piled up a towering 22,895 receiving yards during his career—still the highest total ever recorded! Imagine building a giant skyscraper by stacking yards of football magic. He played for two decades, outlasting and outshining almost everyone who tried to cover him. His secret? Perfect timing, dazzling footwork, and the ability to turn every short pass into a highlight-reel moment. **Takeaway**: When you mix incredible skill with patient practice, you can build a record so tall that no one has been able to climb it since.

Emmitt Smith's Mountain of Rushing Yards

Emmitt Smith, a running back who ran with unstoppable determination, owns a record-setting 18,355 rushing yards. Think of each yard as a tiny building block, and before anyone knew it, he had built a huge mountain no runner has ever matched! Emmitt zipped through defenses, ducked under tacklers, and slipped past linebackers, all while keeping his legs pumping like powerful pistons in a race car engine. **Takeaway**: This teaches us that steady effort—one yard at a time—can create something unbreakable.

Tom Brady's Glittering Chest of Championships

Tom Brady, a quarterback whose calm presence felt like having a super-smart coach right on the field, earned 7 Super Bowl championships—more than any other player in history. It's as if he found a treasure map to victory and followed it again and again! His pinpoint throws, endless focus, and knack for staying cool under the brightest lights helped him lift more championship trophies than anyone imagined possible. **Takeaway**: Tom Brady shows us that when you combine a sharp mind, fearless heart, and belief in yourself, you can keep unlocking success, one shiny trophy at a time.

Don Shula's Tower of Coaching Triumphs

Head coach Don Shula stood at the summit of coaching success with 347 total wins, the most any head coach has ever achieved! He guided teams for decades, shaping players into powerful units and drawing out their very best. His approach blended deep knowledge of the game with a leader's touch, stacking victory after victory like blocks in a never-ending fortress of triumph. **Takeaway**: Don Shula reminds us that great leadership—built from fairness, wisdom, and the courage to push forward—can create achievements that stand tall for generations.

Peyton Manning's Five-Star MVP Streak

Peyton Manning, a quarterback who studied defenses like a puzzle master, earned the Most Valuable Player award 5 times, more than any other player. He knew where each defender would move almost before they did, and he turned that knowledge into touchdown after touchdown. With quick reads, pinpoint passes, and tireless preparation, Manning became the ultimate field general. **Takeaway**: Peyton Manning's record shows that when you learn, prepare, and think ahead, you can outsmart any challenge.

Bruce Smith's Mighty 200 Sack Benchmark

Defensive powerhouse Bruce Smith took down the opposing team's quarterback 200 times, the highest sack total ever recorded! Picture him as a superhero who always burst through blockers at the perfect moment. With roaring speed and booming strength, he made the backfield his personal playground, tackling his way into football history. **Takeaway**: Bruce Smith proves that combining raw strength with laser-focused determination can break barriers and set records that echo through time.

Drew Brees's Unbelievable Passing Accuracy

Drew Brees, a quarterback as accurate as a painter's brush, completed 7,142 passes—more than any other player in history. Each throw was like a magic trick that put the ball exactly where it needed to be, turning ordinary plays into jaw-dropping moments. His remarkable consistency transformed him into the ultimate passing machine, trusted by teammates to deliver the ball perfectly every time. **Takeaway**: Drew Brees shows that precision, careful practice, and aiming for excellence over and over again can turn tough tasks into smooth, graceful success stories.

Brett Favre's Incredible Ironman Streak

Brett Favre, a quarterback who combined grit and guts, started 297 consecutive regular-season games at one point—a streak that's still unmatched! While others sat out with injuries, he pushed through pain and kept going, like a train that never slowed down. This legendary run wasn't about flashy stats, but pure toughness and reliability, game after game. **Takeaway**: Brett Favre teaches us that showing up every day, no matter what challenges appear, can build a legacy of true toughness and perseverance.

Tony Dungy's History-Making Coaching Milestone

Tony Dungy became the first African American head coach to win a Super Bowl, a landmark achievement that changed the way people saw the sport's leaders. He guided his players not with shouting, but with calm support and steady wisdom. By proving greatness could come with kindness, he inspired future generations to believe that anyone's dreams can become reality. **Takeaway**: Tony Dungy's milestone reminds us that when you break down barriers, you open the door for others to follow, making the world a place where everyone's talent can shine.

Football Brain Games And Trivia!

Game 1 – Touchdown True-or-False

Get ready to tackle this fun True-or-False quiz all about American football! You'll answer questions about the rules, how to score, and even some cool history. Some will be easy, and others will challenge you. Mark each statement as T (true) or F (false), then check your answers at the end. If you're not sure about an answer, try thinking about what you've seen in real games or things you've heard while watching.

1 – A standard football field, not counting the end zones, is 100 yards long. ☐ T ☐ F

2 – A touchdown is worth 7 points. ☐ T ☐ F

3 – The football is often called a "pigskin," but today it's usually made of cowhide or synthetic material. ☐ T ☐ F

4 – The National Football League (NFL) is the most popular professional American football league in the world. ☐ T ☐ F

5 – A field goal is worth 2 points. ☐ T ☐ F

6 – Line of scrimmage is an imaginary line that marks where a play starts. ☐ T ☐ F

7 – Each team has 13 players on the field during a play. ☐ T ☐ F

8 – The forward pass was once illegal in American football. ☐ T ☐ F

9 – The shape of the football evolved from early soccer and rugby balls, which were more rounded. ☐ T ☐ F

10 – The Super Bowl is the championship game of the NFL. ☐ T ☐ F

11 – Today, NFL goalposts stand at the goal line. ☐ T ☐ F

12 – A safety, earned by tackling an opponent in their own end zone, is worth 2 points. ☐ T ☐ F

13 – In American football, you score points by shooting the ball into a net. ☐ T ☐ F

14 – Offensive team has two downs to advance the ball at least 10 yards. ☐ T ☐ F

15 – Walter Camp, often called the "Father of American Football," helped shape the modern rules. ☐ T ☐ F

16 – If a player with the ball steps out of bounds, the play ends at that spot. ☐T ☐ F

17 – The NFL was founded after the first Super Bowl took place. ☐ T ☐ F

18 – The first Super Bowl featured the Green Bay Packers and the Kansas City Chiefs. ☐ T ☐ F

19 – On offense, teams try to move the ball downfield to score, while the defense tries to stop them or force a turnover. ☐ T ☐ F

20 – Card draw at the start of the game decides which team gets the ball first. ☐ T ☐ F

21 – In the NFL, the game clock keeps running after most plays unless there's an incomplete pass, a player goes out of bounds, or there's a penalty. ☐ T ☐ F

22 – An NFL game is divided into four quarters, each lasting 15 minutes of game time. ☐ T ☐ F

23 – A "Hail Mary" is a long, last-chance forward pass usually made near the end of a half or a game. ☐ T ☐ F

24 – Referee signals a touchdown by raising left arm straight up in the air. ☐ T ☐ F

25 – The Heisman Trophy is awarded to the most outstanding player in high school football each year. ☐ T ☐ F

26 – The Lombardi Trophy is awarded to the Super Bowl champion. ☐ T ☐ F

Game 2 - Position Pairs Challenge

Introduction

In American football, each player has a unique and vital part to play. The variety of positions you see on the field today has its roots in the sport's transition from rugby-like run-heavy tactics to the modern passing game we know and love. Understanding these positions is an excellent way to appreciate how the entire offense, defense, and special teams work together. In this activity, you'll match seven common football positions to their primary roles. By identifying what each position does, you'll get a better sense of how the entire offense, defense, and special teams collaborate.

The Challenge

Below are two columns: one lists seven positions, and the other lists seven detailed descriptions. Match each position (1–7) to its correct description (A–G). You can draw lines, connect numbers to letters, or fill in the blanks—whatever works best for you.

Hint

Think about each position's main job. Who throws the ball? Who usually runs with it? Who catches? Which players battle in the trenches on each side? Who's known for big tackles, and who is kicking the field goals? Use these clues to guide you.

Position	Which Letter Matches?
Quarterback	→
Running Back	→
Wide Receiver	→
Offensive Lineman	→
Defensive Lineman	→
Linebacker	→
Kicker	→

Descriptions:

A. These players mainly run the ball, especially when only a few yards are needed or a big burst can change the game. They also catch passes and help protect the quarterback, showing off their all-around skills.

B. Often called the "field general," this player stands behind the center to lead the offense. They call plays, read defenses, and throw accurate passes under pressure.

C. Positioned to catch passes downfield, they rely on speed, crisp routes, and good hands to get open. Timing with the quarterback is key, and they must make tough catches—even in tight coverage.

D. These big blockers protect the quarterback and open paths for runners. Using strength, technique, and teamwork, they form a "wall" that keeps the offense safe and moving forward.

E. Lining up near the ball on defense, these players try to stop runs and pressure the quarterback. They use power and technique to break through blocks and disrupt the offense.

F. These defenders tackle ball carriers, cover shorter passes, and sometimes rush the quarterback. Known as the "quarterback of the defense," they call signals, read offenses, and react quickly to every play.

G. Handling kickoffs, extra points, and field goals, this role demands precise technique and calm under pressure. They can swing the score with accurate kicks or pin opponents deep with well-placed kickoffs.

Game 3 – Score It Right

Introduction

Scoring in American football might seem tricky at first, but once you know all the standard point values, you'll be able to keep track of the game in no time! Here's a quick rundown:

Touchdown (TD): **6 points**
Extra Point (after a touchdown): **1 point**
Two-Point Conversion (after a touchdown): **2 points**
Field Goal (FG): **3 points**
Safety: **2 points**

Below, you'll find four scenarios in which two teams, Team A and Team B, score in various ways. For each scenario, follow these steps:

Calculate each team's total points using the point values above. Then, compare the totals to see who wins. We've left space for you to write down your calculations and final scores. Good luck!

Scenario	Team A	Team B
Scenario 1	- 1 Touchdown - 1 Field Goal - 1 Safety	- 2 Touchdowns - 1 Extra Point
Your Calculations	Team A's Score: ____ Team B's Score: ____ Winner: ____	
Scenario 2	- 3 Touchdowns - 2 Extra Points - 1 Field Goal	- 2 Touchdowns - 2 Extra Points - 1 Safety
Your Calculations	Team A's Score: ____ Team B's Score: ____ Winner: ____	
Scenario 3	- 2 Touchdowns - 2 Extra Points - 2 Field Goals	- 1 Touchdown - 1 Extra Point - 3 Field Goals - 1 Safety
Your Calculations	Team A's Score: ____ Team B's Score: ____ Winner: ____	
Scenario 4	- 2 Touchdowns - 2 Extra Points - 1 Safety	- 2 Touchdowns - 1 Extra Point - 1 Two-Point Conversion - 1 Field Goal
Your Calculations	Team A's Score: ____ Team B's Score: ____ Winner: ____	

Game 4 – Word Scramble

American football's language has evolved over decades, with some terms tracing back to rugby. By exploring these words, you'll gain new insight into the game. This word scramble tests your spelling skills while teaching football's unique terminology.

Instructions:

- Write your guess on the line below each scrambled word. Think about offense, defense, and special teams—how these words fit in the game. Remember, some terms have roots in rugby or early versions of football!

    1. **AMGICRMES**

        ○ **Hint**: A rugby-inspired word that's all about starting the action!

        ○ Your Answer: _____

    2. **BAILUDE**

        ○ **Hint**: A quick change called by the quarterback to surprise the defense!

        ○ Your Answer: _____

    3. **GIPKINS**

        ○ **Hint**: A funny name for the football that hints at its wild past!

        ○ Your Answer: _____

    4. **TBILZ**

        ○ **Hint**: A bold move where defenders charge in like a storm!

- Your Answer: _____

5. LUEDDH

- **Hint**: A quick meeting where players gather to discuss the upcoming play.
- Your Answer: _____

6. TNPU

- **Hint**: A strategic kick used to shift field position, typically on fourth down.
- Your Answer: _____

7. AFSETY

- **Hint**: This word can describe a scoring play worth two points if the offense is tackled in its own end zone—or a defensive position on the field.
- Your Answer: _____

8. MIFOONRTA

- **Hint**: The way players on offense or defense line up on the field, setting the stage for each play.
- Your Answer: _____

9. FIFODES

- **Hint**: A penalty called when a player crosses the line of scrimmage too early.
- Your Answer: _____

10. CBTAUHOKC

- **Hint**: This occurs when the ball is downed in the end zone or kicked out of the end zone, preventing a return.
- Your Answer: _____

Game 5 – Name that NFL Team!

INTRODUCTION

Many **NFL** team names carry fascinating stories rooted in history, culture, or local pride. In this brain game, you'll explore seven riddles—each describing an NFL team through its mascot, city, or a special historical link. Your challenge is to figure out <u>*WHICH TEAM*</u> is being described.

THE CORE

Write down your best guess for each in the space provided. If you're stuck, think about **where** each team plays (the city's nickname or history might guide you), the **icon** or **mascot** they use (e.g., a fierce animal, a bird, a historical figure), and **why** it matters to that region (like industry, local legends, or historical events).

1. **RIDDLE #1:** I'm from the "Windy City," and I share my name with a big, strong forest animal.
   My claws and teeth might be scary, but my fans give big hugs in the stands!

   Your Guess:
   _____

2. **RIDDLE #2:** In a town famous for steel, my logo is a trio of diamond shapes. We forge victories just like molten metal for trophies!

   Your Guess:
   _____

3. **RIDDLE #3:** You might say my hometown packs a punch of dairy pride— I was named for the people who worked in a local meat-packing company!

Your Guess:

_____

4. **RIDDLE #4:** I'm named for the frontier spirit and the rugged ranchers of the Old West.

   My star stands for the Lone Star State, where I roam the field in a big hat!

Your Guess:

_____

5. **RIDDLE #5:** My mascot is a regal bird, known for its soaring flight.

   Born in a city that's historically linked to freedom, we spread our wings and fly!

Your Guess:

_____

6. **RIDDLE #6:** My name honors the brave adventurers who rushed west to find gold.

   In a hilly city, we shine bright like the treasure they once sought!

Your Guess:

_____

7. **RIDDLE #7:** My purple warriors nod to an ancient sea-faring people from Northern Europe.

   We sail on the field with horns on our helmets, forging forward in every clash!

Your Guess:

_____

Game 6 – Penalty Decoder

Introduction

In American football, penalties are a vital way to keep the game fair, safe, and fun. When players break the rules—either by moving too early, grabbing opponents illegally, or acting in unsportsmanlike ways—the officials throw a bright yellow flag onto the field. These flags help ensure everyone follows the same guidelines, so every team has an equal chance to succeed. In this game, you'll learn to spot some of the most common penalties simply by decoding their clues!

The Core Puzzle

Below are six short clues describing different penalties. Your job is to match each clue to its proper penalty name from this list: **False Start, Offside, Delay of Game, Unsportsmanlike Conduct, Pass Intereference, Holding.**

1. **Clue A:**

    - *"This penalty occurs when a defensive player crosses the line of scrimmage before the ball is snapped, gaining an unfair advantage."*

    - **Your Answer:** _____

2. **Clue B:**

    - *"This penalty is called when any offensive player moves before the ball is snapped, disrupting the timing of the play."*

    - **Your Answer:** _____

3. **Clue C:**

    ○ *"This penalty is called when a player illegally grabs or restricts an opponent who doesn't have the ball."*

    ○ **Your Answer:** _____

4. **Clue D:**

    ○ *"This penalty happens if the offense takes too long to snap the ball or deliberately stalls the game."*

    ○ **Your Answer:** _____

5. **Clue E:**

    ○ *"This penalty is called when a defender (or occasionally an offensive player) prevents a receiver from having a fair chance to catch a pass."*

    ○ **Your Answer:** _____

6. **Clue F:**

    ○ *"This penalty covers unacceptable behavior on the field—anything from taunting to especially rough hits outside the rules."*

    ○ **Your Answer:** _____

Hint

- Think about who usually commits each penalty (offense vs. defense). Recall that penalties like **Offside** and **False Start** both deal with premature movement—but one is typically for the defense, and the other is for the offense. Penalties such as **Holding** or **Pass Interference** involve direct interaction between players, especially when one is trying to restrict or prevent the other from making a fair play.

Solutions – Basketball Brain Games And Trivia!

Game 1 – Touchdown True-or-False (Solution)

1 – True. The main part of the field is 100 yards long, plus two 10-yard end zones.

2 – False. A touchdown is worth 6 points. After scoring, teams try for an extra point kick (1 point) or a two-point conversion (2 points).

3 – True. "Pigskin" is just a nickname. Modern footballs are usually made of leather from cows or from synthetic materials. *(Early footballs were made from animal bladders.)*

4 – True. NFL is the top professional American football league, watched by millions.

5 – False. A field goal is worth 3 points, not 2.

6 – True. Line of scrimmage is an invisible line where the ball is placed to start each play.

7 – False. Each team sends 11 players onto the field during a play, not 13.

8 – True. Before 1906, the forward pass was not allowed. Allowing it helped make the game safer and more exciting.

9 – True. The ball was once more rounded, like a rugby ball, but it became more oval to make passing easier.

10 – True. The Super Bowl is the NFL's big championship game, played at the end of the season.

11 – False. Goalposts used to be at the goal line, but they were moved to the back of the end zone since 1974 to protect players from running into them.

12 – True. A safety, which can happen if the offense is tackled in their own end zone, gives the defending team 2 points.

13 – False. In football, you don't score by getting the ball into a net. You score by running or catching the ball in the end zone or kicking it through the uprights.

14 – False. The offense gets four tries (downs) to move the ball forward at least 10 yards, not two.

15 – True. Walter Camp helped shape the rules that turned football into what it is today.

16 – True. Stepping out of bounds ends the play right where the player left the field.

17 – False. The NFL was founded in 1920, many years before the first Super Bowl was played in 1967.

18 – True. Super Bowl I (in 1967) was between the Green Bay Packers and the Kansas City Chiefs.

19 – True. The offense tries to score, and the defense tries to stop them. It's a constant battle back and forth.

20 – False. The coin toss at the start decides who gets the ball first or which goal they'll defend, not card draw.

21 – True. The clock stops for things like incomplete passes, going out of bounds, and penalties, making time management very important.

22 – True. An NFL game has four quarters of 15 minutes each, for a total of 60 minutes of game time (not counting stops).

23 – True. A "Hail Mary" is a long, hopeful pass usually thrown as a last attempt to score when time is almost out.

24 – False. The referee raises both arms straight up to signal a touchdown, not left arm only.

25 – False. The Heisman Trophy goes to the top college football player each year, not high school.

26 – True. The Lombardi Trophy, named after Coach Vince Lombardi, is given to the Super Bowl winner.

Game 2 – Position Pairs Challenge (Solution)

Ready to see if you nailed it? Here's how the positions line up!

Position	Which Letter Matches?
Quarterback	→ B
Running Back	→ A
Wide Receiver	→ C
Offensive Lineman	→ D
Defensive Lineman	→ E
Linebacker	→ F
Kicker	→ G

Reflection

- **Which position would you most like to play and why?**
    - Would you take on the quarterback's challenge, making split-second decisions with the game in your hands? Or the wide receiver's thrill of outsmarting defenders with speed and precision? Maybe the kicker's focus, where one kick can decide everything, or the lineman's strength, protecting the team's stars with silent determination. Each position demands unique skills—strategy, power, focus, or teamwork. Use this question to spark a fun discussion about each position's demands and thrills, and discover how every role contributes to the game in its own amazing way!

Game 3 – Score It Right (Solution)

Time to uncover the champions—who scored big and who fell short? Let's find out!

Scenario	Team A	Team B
Scenario 1	1 Touchdown = 6 1 Field Goal = 3 1 Safety = 2 **Total = 11**	2 Touchdowns = 2 × 6 = 12 1 Extra Point = 1 **Total = 13**
Winner	Team B (13 to 11)	
Scenario 2	3 Touchdowns = 3 × 6 = 18 2 Extra Points = 2 × 1 = 2 1 Field Goal = 3 **Total = 23**	2 Touchdowns = 2 × 6 = 12 2 Extra Points = 2 × 1 = 2 1 Safety = 2 **Total = 16**
Winner	Team A (23 to 16)	
Scenario 3	2 Touchdowns = 2 × 6 = 12 2 Extra Points = 2 × 1 = 2 2 Field Goals = 2 × 3 = 6 **Total = 20**	1 Touchdown = 6 1 Extra Point = 1 3 Field Goals = 3 × 3 = 9 1 Safety = 2 **Total = 18**
Winner	Team A (20 to 18)	
Scenario 4	2 Touchdowns = 2 × 6 = 12 2 Extra Points = 2 × 1 = 2 1 Safety = 2 **Total = 16**	2 Touchdowns = 2 × 6 = 12 1 Extra Point = 1 1 Two-Point Conversion = 2 1 Field Goal = 3 **Total = 18**
Winner	Team B (18 to 16)	

Game 4 – Word Scramble (Solution)

Compare your answers below to see if you unscrambled each term correctly. How many did you get right?

1. **SCRIMMAGE** (AMGICRMES)
   - *Definition*: The line of scrimmage is where each play begins, historically adapted from rugby formations.

2. **AUDIBLE** (BAILUDE)
   - *Definition*: A change in the play called verbally by the quarterback just before the ball is snapped.

3. **PIGSKIN** (GIPKINS)
   - *Definition*: A common nickname for the football, originating from the animal-skin coverings used long ago.

4. **BLITZ** (TBILZ)
   - *Definition*: A defensive strategy involving extra players rushing the quarterback with speed and intensity.

5. **HUDDLE** (LUEDDH)
   - *Definition*: A brief gathering where the team discusses the play or strategy before lining up.

6. **PUNT** (TNPU)
   - *Definition*: A specialized kick used to transfer possession downfield when an

offense faces a long-yardage fourth down.

7. **SAFETY** (AFSETY)

   - *Definition*: Can mean two things:

     i. A defensive position in the secondary.

     ii. A 2-point scoring play if the offense is tackled in its own end zone.

8. **FORMATION** (MIFOONRTA)

   - *Definition*: The arrangement of players on the field before the snap, crucial for executing plays effectively.

9. **OFFSIDE** (FIFODES)

   - *Definition*: A penalty called when a defensive (or offensive) player moves beyond the line of scrimmage before the ball is snapped.

10. **TOUCHBACK** (CBTAUHOKC)

    - *Definition*: Occurs when the ball is kicked into or caught in the end zone and is not returned, starting the next play at a predetermined spot (often the 25-yard line in many leagues).

Game 5 – Name that NFL Team! (Solution)

Riddle #1 Answer: Chicago Bears

- They come from Chicago, famously nicknamed the "Windy City."
- "Bears" is a nod to the city's baseball team, the "Cubs," but bigger and tougher!

Originally, the team was called the Decatur Staleys before moving to Chicago and adopting the Bears name.

Riddle #2 Answer: Pittsburgh Steelers

- Hailing from Pittsburgh, a city famed for steel production.
- Their logo features three **hypocycloids** (diamond shapes) symbolizing coal, iron ore, and scrap steel.

The Steelers' name and logo come from the American iron and steel industry that once thrived in Pittsburgh.

Riddle #3 Answer: Green Bay Packers

- They play in Green Bay, Wisconsin—an area known for its dairy and meat-packing industries.
- The team name originated from workers at the Indian Packing Company.

The Packers are uniquely **publicly owned**, making fans literal shareholders in the team.

Riddle #4 Answer: Dallas Cowboys

- They represent the independent, adventurous spirit of Texas—"The Lone Star State."

- Their star logo is a direct nod to that single star on the Texas flag.

The "cowboy" persona reflects the rugged ranchers and frontier heroes of the Old West, an iconic symbol of Texas culture.

Riddle #5 Answer: Philadelphia Eagles

- Eagles are regal birds, and the bald eagle is a symbol of American ideals.

- Philadelphia is a city deeply connected to American history and freedom (think Liberty Bell!).

Legend says the Eagles' name was partly inspired by the "Blue Eagle," a symbol from the 1930s New Deal program—but the bold bird still perfectly suits this city of independence.

Riddle #6 Answer: San Francisco 49ers

- Named after the fortune-seekers of the 1849 Gold Rush in California.

- San Francisco is famously hilly, and gold remains a key part of their color scheme.

The name "49ers" commemorates the spirit of adventure and determination shown by early gold prospectors.

Riddle #7 Answer: Minnesota Vikings

- The name celebrates the region's strong Scandinavian heritage.

- The Vikings' mascot and horned helmets recall the legendary Norse explorers (even if real Vikings probably didn't use horned helmets!).

Game 6 – Penalty Decoder (Solution)

Solution (Check Your Answers!)

1. **Clue A → Offside**
   - *When a defensive player lines up or moves across the line of scrimmage before the snap.*

2. **Clue B → False Start**
   - *When an offensive player moves too early, causing the play to halt before it begins.*

3. **Clue C → Holding**
   - *Illegally grabbing or restricting an opponent who is not in possession of the ball.*

4. **Clue D → Delay of Game**
   - *Failing to snap the ball in time or intentionally slowing the game's progress.*

5. **Clue E → Pass Interference**
   - *Illegally hindering a receiver's opportunity to catch a forward pass.*

6. **Clue F → Unsportsmanlike Conduct**
   - *Any rude, dangerous, or out-of-line behavior that violates the spirit of fair play.*

Afterword

Hey, gridiron greats! We've reached the final whistle of our football adventure. From Jerry Rice's unmatched precision to Patrick Mahomes' game-changing plays, and Reggie White's unstoppable force on defense, we've celebrated the players who redefined the sport. Along the way, we uncovered amazing football facts, explored historic rivalries, and solved brain-teasing trivia that tested your football IQ.

So, what's next, future MVP? Will you make the winning catch, strategize the perfect play as a coach, or become the voice of football as a commentator? No matter where your journey takes you, remember the lessons these legends taught us: work hard, dream big, and play every down with heart and determination.

The field is yours—go make history!

Harris Baker

Also by Harris Baker

Discover More Stories by Harris Baker – Just Scan Below!

For partnerships or collaboration inquiries, contact me at

harrisbakerpublishing@gmail.com

www.ingramcontent.com/pod-product-compliance
Lightning Source LLC
Chambersburg PA
CBHW070634030426
42337CB00020B/4006